Bailey's book is timely and wonderful. It will touch you deeply in addressing women's needs and longing for companionship and intimacy with friends. She shows clearly how to make this possible by applying practical and insightful ideas. I loved this book, and I think you will too!

SALLY CLARKSON, author, encourager, friend, podcast host of *At Home with Sally*

Bailey Hurley has written a remarkable book that has the power to transform not only how you *view* friendship but how you *do* friendship. Brimming with Christ-centered joy and exuberance, Bailey takes you by the hand (as any friend should) and helps you navigate the often-overwhelming terrain of friendships in the modern world. One part guide, one part friend cheerleader, Bailey is the friend we all wish lived next door (and who we could grab a mug of coffee with). But more than that, Bailey ultimately directs our gaze and affections to our truest friend—Jesus Christ. Grab this book today and get motivated because friendships have the power to make a scary and lonely world a little less frightening and a whole lot more inviting.

JONATHAN D. HOLMES, author of *The Company We Keep*, executive director of Fieldstone Counseling

Bailey Hurley's book *Together Is a Beautiful Place* is a thoughtful resource for those of us who want to make— and develop—Christ-centered friendships. Through sharing her own story (full of friendship victories *and* failures), Bailey offers practical tools and spiritual insights so we can cultivate true friendships that flow from the love of Christ.

> ANN SWINDELL, founder of Writing with Grace, author of *The Path to Peace* and *Still Waiting*

Having known Bailey personally for many years, I trust her friendship advice. She knows how to show up, love, and serve! Bailey gently but boldly names the fears that hinder healthy relationships, but she doesn't leave us stuck in that lonely place—she puts tools in our hands to help us become committed girlfriends, freely giving and receiving the friendship we crave. She helped me realize that my friendships aren't just about me, about my satisfaction or fulfillment: This is about Kingdom building, one intimate connection at a time.

> AMY LIVELY, author of *How to Love Your Neighbor Without Being Weird*

Bailey beautifully illustrates the power of togetherness and the importance of building life-giving connections in *Together Is a Beautiful Place*. Through her masterful demonstration of building an inclusive table, she reminds us all that genuine relationships are within our grasp, even when community building feels out of reach.

By sharing her own extremely relatable journey of friendship fumbles, she powerfully showcases how meaningful friendships are cultivated, not wished into existence. Deep, long-lasting relationships require intentionality, and Bailey gives us a blueprint to better understand what it really takes to cultivate meaningful connections when each of us inevitably finds ourselves in a season where it's time to make friends again. If you've ever struggled with building a close-knit community, this book is for you. If you have lifelong friends you cherish but find yourself wondering how the heck to make the most of your time in maintaining friendships, this book is for you. We all long for a table with a spot reserved just for us, and Bailey tells us how in *Together Is a Beautiful Place*.

KELSEY CHAPMAN, author of *What They Taught Me*

With lots of heart and gospel truth, Bailey invites us into a safe space to consider the essential topic of friendship. Let *Together Is a Beautiful Place* remind you of Christ's compassion for every woman, motivate you toward a right understanding of sacrificial living in friendships, and call you to more in relating to one another in kindness, just as it did for me.

HOLLY MACKLE, author of *Little Hearts, Prepare Him Room*, curator of *Same Here, Sisterfriend*

There is a big difference between a social life and truly being in community—and if it's the latter that you want, Bailey will inspire you step-by-step on that journey. With poignant honesty and contagious hope, Bailey guides us all to the deeper friendships we're made to experience.

SHASTA NELSON, MDIV, friendship expert, author of *Frientimacy*

We all crave meaningful connection, but we often struggle with how to make and keep authentic relationships. Now more than ever, we need a mentor like Bailey Hurley to come alongside us with godly wisdom and practical advice. *Together Is a Beautiful Place* is a must-read for women of all ages and stages in life.

KRISTIN SCHELL, author of *The Turquoise Table*

Truth be told, I seldom read nonfiction books by authors less than half my age—the generational gap in life experiences is too wide. In *Together Is a Beautiful Place*, however, Bailey Hurley winsomely offers fresh yet timeless principles on friendship building that I have found to be true in nearly seven decades of life. We are never too old to discover new friends who can become the old friends we long to have. I'm thankful to Bailey for pointing the way to rich relationships for a new generation.

MAGGIE WALLEM ROWE, author of *This Life We Share*

TOGETHER IS A BEAUTIFUL PLACE

Together
is a
Beautiful
Place

FINDING, KEEPING, AND LOVING OUR FRIENDS

BAILEY T. HURLEY

A NavPress resource published in alliance
with Tyndale House Publishers

NavPress is the publishing ministry of The Navigators, an international Christian organization and leader in personal spiritual development. NavPress is committed to helping people grow spiritually and enjoy lives of meaning and hope through personal and group resources that are biblically rooted, culturally relevant, and highly practical.

For more information, visit NavPress.com.

For information about special discounts for bulk purchases, please contact Tyndale House Publishers at csresponse@tyndale.com, or call 1-855-277-9400.

ISBN 978-1-64158-316-9

Printed in the United States of America

28	27	26	25	24	23	22
7	6	5	4	3	2	1

To Hunter, Liv, and Henri:

May you pursue the kind of friendships that make a meaningful life.

CONTENTS

TOGETHER IS BETTER

You know things are bad when you have to lie to your mom about having friends.

As my first year of college drew to a close, I—unlike my classmates—could not wait to pack up and head home for summer. My mom, aunt, and cousin had traveled all the way from Kansas to California to drive me home. I was a basket case the entire two days they were there helping me pack. The stress of finishing finals, organizing my room, and coming to terms with the year ending loomed over me.

School and extracurriculars had made it easy to avoid thinking about how lonely my freshman year had been, but with my family there asking questions? The truth about my lack of new friendships was sinking in.

When I had finished my last final, packed my last oversized college hoodie, and checked out with my RA, I met my family by the car to leave. It was dark outside when we pulled out of the campus parking lot. But before we could exit, my mom suddenly stopped the car.

"Why don't you say good-bye to all your friends?" she said. "Take as much time as you need. I'll wait here in the car until you're ready."

I closed the car door slowly and gave her a slight nod. As I walked toward the row of freshman dorms, tears began to form in my eyes. I would have no long, drawn-out good-byes.

First, I visited my roommate. She had been my one saving grace that year, the person I could count on. We'd shared late-night pillow talks and binge-eaten popcorn in our beds. She understood, too, the challenges of creating community. We were two misfits who had found one another, a blessing neither of us recognized at the time. Before we said good-bye, we signed our initials on the top of our door to prove we had survived this first year, then hugged and went our separate ways. We would be studying abroad in different countries the following year and wouldn't see each other for eight months.

Then, as I stepped out of our dorm and onto the lawn, I saw all these groups of friends—crying, laughing, promising to stay connected.

Yes, I'd had a wonderful roommate. But I still felt like I was missing something: I longed for a friend group that had never materialized. The feeling of "left out" sunk in deep as I watched other girls hug each other close. Why was I so unlucky at building a group of friends?

I stalled outside the dorms so it would seem like I'd been busy exchanging addresses and agreeing to visit soon.

Then I went back to the car and lied to my mom: "Yes, I had lots of quality hugs and fought off a trail of friends just to make it back to the car." And we drove off.

The whole drive home, I wondered, *Is there something wrong with me?* Friendship hadn't always felt this hopeless. At one point in my life, my relationships had been so deep and meaningful that friendship had been my whole world. Why couldn't I figure out friendship at this life stage?

If only female friendship were as uncomplicated as finding playmates on the first day of kindergarten.

FINDING FRIENDSHIP

Look at sweet little Bailey, with that toothless grin and those pink GAP jellies. Up until now, her friendship selection had been scarce, though she likely didn't know any better.

Now, as an adult of toddlers myself, I recognize that my prekindergarten pals were the kids of my mother's friends—aka "forced friendships." If my mother wanted to meet up with her gal pals who also had kids, then we were expected to play nicely together, whether we liked each other or not.

But kindergarten Bailey was finally ready to make friends all on her own.

Or maybe not?

What you can't see in that picture is my mind churning through all the potential pitfalls of a new, unscripted friendship setting: *What if everyone thinks I smell funny? What if no one talks to me?* And the biggest question: *Will anyone want to be my friend?*

Even at five, I feared no one would want me in their inner circle.

But on my first day of kindergarten, as I stepped into the classroom, a blonde-haired girl ran up to me. I remember standing close to my mom as the teacher tried to get me to pronounce her last name (O'Hearn wasn't an easy name to say!). I was overwhelmed by all the kids who looked like they already were comfortable working on other activities together. How was I going to insert myself into their play? Yet this sweet girl, without any inhibition, left the small blue table where other kids had already gathered to color and approached *me*.

"Do you want to color with me?"

Invitations like these are some of the most profound and important words a young child will ever hear.

Because that simple invitation meant: *You like me! You don't even know me, but you are willing to give this friendship thing a chance.* She took the first steps to invite me into her world, and by the end of the day, we told our moms we were "best friends." That brave blonde girl and I did indeed become best friends, and twenty-five years later, we've been through the bridesmaid and baby stages of life together.

Picture proof that we made it:

But the days of elementary friend-ships gave way to more complicated adolescent times. Emotions, puberty, unfortunate fashion . . . friendship was more involved than coloring together. Our friend circles were tight-knit because we spent eight-plus hours a day, five days a week together (with some sleepovers sprinkled in). Consistency is a powerful connector.

Play-based friendship turned into activity-based friendship, where our busy schedules aligned with tennis practice, the school musical, and prom. Unlikely friendships were forged over late-night test preps and whispers about how cute the senior lead was in his drama costume.

During high school, I also became more involved in my local youth group, a community of guys and girls that changed my life forever. Our friendships weren't tied to a sport that finished after a season, or a club that met for a few weeks—these relationships were rich and deep, founded on our love for Jesus. Our faith is what brought us together, a mutual pursuit of understanding how our gifts and God's plans intertwined that would transcend all the typical foundations for friendship. We were inseparable.

And then—college. Suddenly it was up to me to find solid besties amongst literally thousands.

Gone were the days when decorating the senior float was the only item on my agenda. I wasn't sure how to navigate making new friends in an environment where I could also choose to focus on school, work, extracurriculars, rest, or YouTube videos.

But surely—because we all lived together in the same community—we would all be on the same page and like the same things. The relationships would flow so naturally, friends would turn into sisters.

I hadn't grasped the reality of what it took to go from strangers to best friends. I didn't realize that meaningful relationships had to be made, not stumbled into.

So, instead of introducing myself to other people in my classes, I kept to myself. I waited for other girls to initiate a night out to grab dinner. I focused on my schoolwork and Skyped friends back home. There was no method to my friend making.

By my junior year, I was *still* in a friendship deficit. I wasn't just lonely—I was depressed. My parents were worried about me. I stopped talking to my friends from back home because it was too painful to hear about their new friendships while I was still at ground zero.

So I tried to find a solution. *Maybe I just need to go do things*, I thought.

I started not just participating in but *leading* Bible studies for different on-campus ministries. I signed up for every exercise class, sorority event, and talent show. If there was a service project, I volunteered. If there was a musical to see, I was in the front row.

Here's the thing I learned: You can be busy with people and still miss the mark for meaningful friendship.

One evening in the middle of my junior year, my sorority was participating in an on-campus dance competition. I'd like to think that in another life, I'd be a professional hip-hop dancer. So even though I wasn't close to anyone attending, I looked forward to watching some killer dance moves and connecting with some of my sorority sisters.

The cafeteria had been transformed into a dance-competition stage that could rival any ABC-show production, and there, front and center, were my sorority sisters. I had to make my way through a crowd of people to reach them, and it took all the social courage I had to act like I belonged.

Earlier in the day, I had given myself a pep talk: *Be more outgoing. Be cheerful. Try to make conversation.* I mentally repeated this mantra as I approached the group of women.

Your sorority sisters are supposed to be your best friends—a group tied together through the bond of "sisterhood." Other women in my sorority found future roommates, bridesmaids, and lifelong friends among the group. I just found it uncomfortable to be in their presence.

Yet, here I was, faking self-confidence and making small talk. I started asking one girl questions about school, and she answered politely—until a friend of hers approached. She quickly turned her back on me and pretended like I wasn't there, almost like she was embarrassed to be discovered talking to me.

Ouch! Rejection hurts. Her actions, whether mean-spirited or unintentional, affirmed the message I'd been fighting against this whole time: that I was unwanted. I felt there was no chance I could redeem this lonely season.

I began to question whether there was something wrong with me.

Then I criticized others, thinking maybe they were the problem.

Finally, I blamed God. There was something wrong with Him. God had led me out onto the cliff of a new city, new college, new community, and then left me all alone. I didn't just feel alone at college—I felt like God had forsaken *our* friendship.

The enemy had my full attention. He whispered in my ear:

No one gets you.

No one wants to be your friend.

God has forgotten you.

Nobody understands what you're going through.

Be angry and discontent with God, but pretend everything is fine.

Hide your loneliness. Keep it to yourself because no one will like a girl who feels out of place.

I believed the lies. So, instead of pressing into community, I avoided it. As long as I was doing something, I didn't have to slow down and feel my loneliness.

I couldn't feel unseen if I was busy doing other things.

I couldn't feel rejected if I was the first one to cancel plans to meet new friends because it was easier to stay home and peruse Anthropologie's new denim line.

I couldn't feel unwanted if no one knew the real me.

Isolating myself felt easier than confronting my insecurities and fears and the lies I'd been believing.

THE HARD TRUTH ABOUT CONNECTION

As it turns out, friendship struggles don't disappear in adulthood. The older we get, the less we find ourselves spending time in the company of good friends. Organic friendship becomes nearly impossible, and the discrepancy between *what we want* in a friendship and *what we have* can be frustrating. There are so many things that make us feel lonely, like getting discouraged by shallow connections or struggling to find your place amid a friend group you've known for years.

If you have found yourself desperately wanting connec-

tion but confused on why you are not experiencing it—
you are not alone. In 2018, a survey by the Kaiser Family
Foundation found that over 22 percent of Americans
feel isolated and left out, lacking meaningful companionship.[1]

And Millennials are the loneliest generation to date.
When YouGov surveyed Americans, they found that
Millennials are most likely to report that they have zero
friends or no close friends.[2] The reason why is unclear, but
one reporter speculates: "Millennials are the first generation raised with schedules that included plenty of extra-
curricular activities and little free time . . . Making and
maintaining friendships requires spending time, and if you
feel like every waking moment must be filled, that can be
difficult."[3]

Others have speculated that the increase of social media
has heightened some of our relational issues of comparison
and the fear of missing out.[4] If we perceive others to have
the perfect friend group we begin to wonder why ours is
lacking—feeding our lonely thoughts.

And lately, I have been asking the question: Have we
moved from avoiding being alone to glorifying solitude? The
memes that joke about staying at home in your sweatpants
and relaxing with a glass of wine or viral videos of adults

joking about their lack of social life give us all permission to say, "Hey, I guess it's okay if I never leave the house again." Are we creating a culture that believes being alone is a privilege, despite our epidemic of loneliness?

All these things are leaving us depressed, dissatisfied, and utterly hopeless in our search for meaningful, lasting friendship.

One of the issues with my pursuit of real friendships in college was that I couldn't tell the difference between my perceived loneliness and actual aloneness. Some people filled me up, while others left me empty. Often, in a crowded space, I felt utterly alone. I had no words to understand what I was experiencing and no tools to change my narrative. Instead of turning my disappointment into a positive, I isolated myself. Instead of looking outward, I caved inward. Instead of being genuine, I was flaky and distrustful. I was closed off to intimacy and immediately judged other women for insignificant reasons. I was my own worst enemy at making friends: I told myself I wanted close-knit friends but was unwilling to extend myself for real connection.

As Christians, how do we reconcile all these friendship disappointments with our innate, God-given longing for closeness?

CHOOSING ROOTED COMMUNITY

God planned for us to glorify Him in community. As soon as God placed Adam in the garden, He saw "it is not good that the man should be alone."[5] How would God know? Possibly because He has only known a shared relationship between Father, Son, and Holy Spirit—communing together is who God is. Unfortunately, our relationships wouldn't stay this way; our longing remained while our connections with God and with other people were broken.

But God had a plan to restore His relationship with us and our relationships with each other. He knew these relationships weren't going to find peace and unity with the snap of a finger. It was going to take a powerful example of sacrifice and love to make healthy, working relationships a possibility this side of heaven. By reconciling the world through Jesus' death and resurrection, we now have the opportunity for a real, intimate relationship with God—as well as sincere, gospel driven friendships.

The connection and longing that we all talk about is also Jesus' desire for His people. In John 17, Jesus intercedes for His believers and asks God for them to "become perfectly one" just like He and the Father are one.[6] Wow! Togetherness is a beautiful bond Jesus invites us into so we experience the goodness of these relationships *and* witness to a world hungry for authentic connection. True friendship is not just a silly idea in your head, or just for those of us who get lucky enough to find it; it is for all of God's people. And God has provided us with a history of people who sought to live in this "oneness," to reflect God's perfect union, a legacy of saints who modeled godly relationships that are

- driven by the love of God;
- committed to shared time together; and
- joined by a mutual purpose.

Acts 2:42-47 shows us one of the church's best examples for godly fellowship. This community is devoted to the apostles' teaching: to knowing God and laying the groundwork for godly relationships. They had Communion together, they prayed together, they experienced miracles together, they praised God together, thus, they *grew* together. Their bond was tied by Jesus but strengthened by *consistent and meaningful time together*.

And God still uses simple daily moments of communing together to create a Spirit-filled group of friends. Sharing meals, meeting needs, reading God's Word, and praying together may not seem like a recipe for creating lasting friendship, but in the time described in Acts, those everyday things made a purposeful community that gave light to the rest of the world. People saw the magic that was happening, and God "added to their number."[7] God chose relationships as our greatest form of influence.

If you are reading this and you think: *I should have had this friendship thing figured out years ago*, then you are in the right place. Building authentic friendships is a practice of little by little. Taking faithful steps towards the type of friendships that move beyond the surface and into the rich soil of life together will create the life-giving relationships you have longed for. Genuine friendship is within your grasp.

Paul's prayer to the Ephesian community is my prayer for you, "that Christ may dwell in your hearts through faith—that you, being rooted and grounded in love, may have strength . . . to know the love of Christ."[8] The first step to growing these "rooted in Jesus" friendships starts with seeing the potential for community and laying down our fears, misplaced priorities, and weariness to love others.

When I moved to Denver right after college graduation, I was on a mission to get friendship right. By developing my friendship with Jesus, I was ready to put aside my misguided ideas of community and choose to be tethered to God's view of community.

Flash-forward a decade, and all the progress I've made to combat my friendship struggles still comes with setbacks. As a wife and mom of three kids, my schedule can be a real hindrance to girl time! My insecurities and the comparison trap make me judgmental and incapable of loving people in my community. Sometimes, pure selfishness sneaks in and lying in bed, watching TV just seems better than spending time with a friend.

Let's not be surprised by the obstacles.

We will find ourselves in a variety of seasons where being a friend will feel like just another thing on our to-do list.

Perhaps the intimidation of moving to a new place and having to start friendships over again paralyzes you.

Or being a newlywed and wanting time with your husband tempt you to put time with your girlfriends on the back burner.

Maybe you are struggling with shame over a friendship breakup.

Or you find yourself in the middle of big work projects and you haven't been able to call your friend back in weeks.

There is never a good time for the hard work of building meaningful friendships.

Intentionality in our friendships means we carefully

consider how we will create *meaningful* connection. It means we recognize that friendships don't "just happen."

Meaningful, lasting friendship is near. God cares about you, and He has provided women right where you are. Maybe your potential friend is in your neighborhood book club, serves alongside you at church, or attends the same gym class. She may live right down the block, or she has a kid in your son's class.

We don't have to search the globe for these potential sisters—we just need to learn how to see them, invest in them, and develop those relationships. No matter our age, we need to be forever students in the art of friendship.

LONGING FOR BELONGING

My hope is that we all can tackle friendship the way my friend bravely approached me on that fateful day at the coloring table. She recognized that doing something together was better than doing it alone.

Since each one of us is called to connect, we can lay down our social anxieties, trusting that Jesus has created opportunities for us to experience thriving friendships. I'm not sure what your friendship journey has been up to this moment, but this is your permission to start over or begin meaningful friendship for the first time.

It's not too late to find where you belong and discover that together is a beautiful place to be.

FRIENDSHIP PEP TALK:
A Toast to Friendship

- *To the girl who is feeling left out or lonely*: You are valued and worthy of a great friendship. Finding community can be challenging, but Jesus is walking with you through these ups and downs. Please hold on for the right friend.

- *To the girl whose social calendar is full*: Keep loving your people well and inviting meaningful connection. But don't get so caught up in the doing that you forget to be you among your trusted friends.

- *To the girl who is hurting or feels betrayed*: Take time to heal. Don't rush to cut others down, but come freely to the safety of Jesus, who knows what rejection feels like.

He will redeem those scars in time, and you will find the courage to trust new friends again.

- *To the mom who isn't sure how to stay in the friendship game*: It's okay to slow down. Perhaps this new pace will be even better for your friendships. Find those two or three friends, and do what you can to stay in touch.

- *To the new girl*: You don't need to find ten new best friends on your first day! Diligently pray and practice good friendship habits to build solid connections a little every day.

- *To the hostess with the mostest*: Thank you for creating opportunities for people to gather. But . . . are you tired? Burned out? Even though you may be a master at inviting people into your home, make sure you carve out time to invite Jesus into your heart.

- *To female friend groups everywhere*: You are not just a social club. You are Kingdom builders, and your friendships are here to reflect God's gospel love and truth. Don't be shocked when community requires you to give much. God has given everything you need to see these friendships through.

- Here's to building meaningful, lasting friendships one day at a time!

1

WORTHY OF FRIENDSHIP

Letting God Reorient Our Thoughts

My first year in Denver, I was navigating community as a student at Denver Seminary. On top of all the classes, I was part of a mentorship seminar. The goal was for students to periodically meet with a faculty mentor and spiritual mentors to work through some of your heart struggles amid the stress of school. At the time, my main struggle was building friendships. Despite my new resolution to "do friendship differently," I carried my previous mistakes with me, and it was hard to fully shake off insecurities around making new friends.

My faculty mentor had a superpower (also known as a spiritual gift): She could see right through her students' facade. This woman could speak directly to a person's heart, which meant I couldn't hide my loneliness from her like I had from trusted adults in the past.

One afternoon, she called me into her office, opened her Bible to John 15, and pushed it in front of me. She asked me to read the first few verses out loud and to pause on verse four.

"Abide in me, and I in you," I read. "As the branch cannot bear fruit by itself, unless it abides in the vine, neither can you, unless you abide in me."

She looked at me, then asked, "Who bears the fruit, Bailey?"

I stared at the Bible, and the inky black words started to blur. I avoided eye contact, looking anywhere else but at her—around her room, at the crosses on the wall, at the candle she left burning on top of her filing cabinet.

"The branches?" I asked nervously.

She shook her head. "Bailey, read it again."

This time I had to concentrate. There it was. "It's the vine. The vine bears the fruit."

"Exactly. Who are you?"

"I'm the branch."

"Who is Jesus?"

"The vine. He is the vine."

She smiled. "Do you see? You are not the one who bears the fruit in your relationships, Bailey. Jesus does that work. You are to abide in Him. Your role is to make time for Him and to rest in His love. You will not have the full life that you want if you try to do everything on your own. You will fail. You think you understand His love, but you still walk around as if you had chains on your hands, enslaved to your past friendship mistakes and your avoidance of failure. Let it go. You are free. He has chosen you to love, not the other way around. Understand how much God loves for you to love others."

The tears were flowing. She had hit the nail on the head. I was still a slave to all the lies the enemy held over me. I had yet to experience God's complete acceptance of me and believe I was worthy of life-giving friendship.

THE THOUGHTS IN OUR HEADS

Friendships begin in our heads. The stories we tell ourselves about who we are or whose we are, significantly impact how we live. What you think about who you are as a friend—according to the stories you replay in your head—significantly changes the way you approach friendships.

If you experience friendship conflict after friendship conflict, you may be telling yourself, *It is not worth my time to pursue friends; they only end in disaster.* If you have had unhealthy friendships, you may be telling yourself, *Having close friends is not a safe endeavor. Opening up to other women was a mistake I will avoid making in the future.* Or you may be stuck forcing expectations on new friends, bringing narratives to the friendship that aren't necessarily bad but set us up for disappointment when people don't act the way we expect them to.

As I pursued new friendships in Denver, I thought only one thing: *These friendships should be like my hometown friendships. Anything different means they are not real friendships.* I had allowed my narrative to control how I viewed the new friends, and it completely ruined my chances of building healthy, real friendships. And when I didn't succeed at first, instead of "try, try, again," I chose the narrative: *I am a failure at making friends.*

Identifying our negative narratives and replacing them with what God says is true about us and about community changes the friend-making experience. As Jon Acuff says in his book *Soundtracks*, "Take out a broken soundtrack. Ask, 'What's the opposite of this?' And then write down the answer."[1] In other words, instead of believing absolutes like

I will ALWAYS feel this way, Friendship will NEVER work out for me, or *No one will EVER like me*, we can try flipping the narrative.

So, instead of approaching a new friendship with *They won't like that I am a homebody because no one ever does*, flip that: *What if this is the person who loves all my quirks and wants to watch all of* Friday Night Lights *for the second time with me?* When we twist our negative narratives into positives, we move our minds to expect genuine connection.

Of course, it's not always so simple. We all know that thoughts like these cannot always be positively explained away:

I just can't stop thinking about how I messed up in the friendship.

I just can't stop feeling unwanted, even if friends invite me places.

I just can't stop believing that I am too much for my friends and no one will want to know the real me.

Take a moment and remember the last time you made a new friend. What fears were playing in your head? What thoughts kept you from being excited and open? Remember, what you believe about yourself privately is what you believe about yourself always. Becoming aware of your negative thoughts is the first step toward opening yourself up to new approaches for friendship. Let's choose courage to dig deep and find the narratives that hold us back from authentic friendship.

Because there's a way to fight them—and a way to win.

FIGHT THE NARRATIVES

The enemy hates healthy, God-honoring friendships. He wants to destroy anything good that God creates, including the good relationships we have—and he does this by drawing us away from truth and down into those thought spirals that keep us from moving forward in our friendships.

When you feel like you've been stuck in a cycle of start-stop friendships, it isn't because you have done something wrong or you are a flop at friendship. The enemy is waging war on your greatest gospel influence—your direct relationships.

But this is the truth of the gospel: You are worthy of friendship because Jesus, the King of kings, died so you could experience the best friendship of all, with the Creator of the universe. The true things God says about His people heal the lies we believe about ourselves. When we first choose to prioritize our relationship with God and believe what He says, we can experience uninhibited friendship—because we have left our friendship baggage at the cross.

The enemy doesn't play fair. But we start to fight back when we let God reveal the enemy's lies for what they are.

Several years ago, I was seeing a counselor regularly because I was having some deep friendship insecurity. When I was surrounded by a certain group of people at my church (who were older, cooler, and wiser), I felt so inadequate, and my insecurity stunted the relationships. I thought everyone didn't like me (and when I stood in a corner quietly, I probably wasn't winning anyone over). I could not get out of my head! I needed some serious healing that could only come from the ultimate Healer.

Being in God's presence is where we can find the genuine love and acceptance God has for us. We find ourselves not only cognitively thinking that we are loved but *actually experiencing love.* When we stop to be with God, we remember that our core identity is *beloved by God.*

When we understand that we are beloved, we no longer have to chase after what we think our friends want from us. We can rest in who God says we are. We can slow down to be loved and even enjoy the process of growing in relationships with others.

Understanding our own belovedness is how we find the courage to invite people into a safe space to connect with us—whether our time together takes place in the parking lot of Target or the prayer room at church. We can be secure in the love we have received and give it away freely without the spiral of thoughts that hold us back.

Theologian and author Henri Nouwen understood the profound implications of this new identity as beloved:

> When we claim and constantly reclaim the truth
> of being the chosen ones, we soon discover within
> ourselves a deep desire to reveal to others their
> own chosenness. Instead of making us feel that we
> are better, more precious or valuable than others,
> our awareness of being chosen opens our eyes to
> the chosenness of others. That is the great joy of
> being chosen: the discovery that others are chosen
> as well.[2]

Or, to put it another way: Since "God so loved us, we also ought to love one another."[3]

When we understand our own belovedness and start to see the belovedness of others, spending time with God is no longer a box on our to-do list; it equips us for quality friendship. It's not just "a thing." It's "*the* thing."

So, my counselor asked me to begin writing down (1) what was actually true about the situation and (2) what solid God truth was present in each of those socially anxious moments. What were the facts of a specific conversation or the way I was greeted when I walked in the door? When I took my emotions and assumptions out of it, I could see that things were okay. When I reminded myself that God is always with me and never leaves me, it made me feel less alone in these intimidating situations. These people did not hate me. I was just so worked up because my false narratives told me that my age and experience made me "less than," which wasn't the case at all.

Making room for God to overwhelm our hearts creates more room for us to see a friend situation with clarity and kindness—for ourselves and other people. And trusting God helps us give ourselves the grace and the opportunity to mess up. That's right. Instead of believing we've already made too many mistakes to have friends, living in belovedness means we get to go in believing this is our chance to find our people. We get to step into each potential friendship anew, showing people who we really are and trusting they will appreciate what makes us unique.

This is what you get to do as the beloved of God: Go into new situations believing that God created you for friendship, that you are worthy of friendship, and that someone out there is looking for a friend just like you.

GRACE IN THE PROCESS

Anything can trigger negative thoughts. Maybe a friend jokes that you tell long-winded stories, and the next thing you know, you are thinking about four years ago, when a mean girl told you that you are boring when you talk, and nobody likes your stories.

Negative thoughts are waiting for their moment to strike. There will be many moments when this process feels like two steps forward and three steps back. When you are struggling, get back on your knees and ask God to heal these broken thoughts. Ask Him to send encouragement through a text or call from an old friend. Many times when I have felt lonely and asked God to show up to get me out of my funk, a friend has called that day, asking to hang out. Please, please don't think that your past friendship fails dictate your future friendship wins. Leaning into God's friendship with us gives us the confidence to seek genuine connection.

Living in the beauty of togetherness is our main objective, and believing truth for ourselves allows us to help others fight their negative narratives too. No one asked us to fight the negative thought battles alone. Offer truth when you see a friend could use it. Remind her of her belovedness, and don't be afraid to share when you have been stuck in unhealthy thought patterns around a friendship situation. Remember: "Two are better than one, because they have a good reward for their toil. For if they fall, one will lift up his fellow. But woe to him who is alone when he falls and has not another to lift him up!"[4]

FRIEND-DATE IDEA:
Coffee-Shop Crawl

I know many find the "coffee date" cliché . . . but when we are honest with ourselves, most of us will admit that we love to sit and catch up with girlfriends over fancy coffee drinks and croissants (#carbsandcommunity is my perfect pairing!).

During my first "adult" summer job, my supervisor insisted that our team meet at a different coffee shop each week. The very first meeting, she bounded inside the coffee shop (possibly already hyped-up on caffeine) with a slip of paper with a rating scale from one to five, with one being the ickiest and five being the ideal coffee experience:

- coffee/tea
- ambience
- baked goods
- bathrooms
- affordability
- music

And of course, a comments section.

At the end of three months and twelve unique coffee-shop visits later, she tallied the results and

MY COFFEE SHOP CRAWL

COFFEE/TEA	1	2	3	4	5
AMBIENCE	1	2	3	4	5
BAKED GOODS	1	2	3	4	5
BATHROOMS	1	2	3	4	5
AFFORDABILITY	1	2	3	4	5
MUSIC	1	2	3	4	5

announced which coffee shop came out on top. (We had all selected this funky shop that had the cheapest but yummiest jumbo cookies.) She also gave us back our rating sheets so we could reread what we had written and laugh at each other's comments.

Out of this experience, I created a coffee-shop crawl for friends who were visiting Denver. This way we could eat good treats, catch up, and get caffeine from all over the city . . . not just the place around the corner from my house. I chose five varied coffee shops, and we visit two or three a day. I bring along the rating sheets, and we fill them out and tally them up at the end so they can go home and tell their local friends which Denver coffee shop is their favorite. Friends enjoy seeing different areas of the city and getting a better feel for what life is like in Denver. And coffee shops are a fun setting to talk and talk and talk.

This is something you could also do with your local friends or with a Bible-study group. Rotating through different coffee shops allows you to see various parts of your community and connect with your friends. If you're looking for good conversation, funky atmospheres, and friend time, try a creative take on the coffee date!

2

FRIENDSHIP FILTERS

Knowing Yourself, Finding Your People

Have you ever tried to search for an item online and gotten so overwhelmed by the hundreds of options? I definitely have, many times. I get so worn out scanning through page after page, I get a bit short with my husband, Tim, as he leans over my shoulder offering suggestions. (I love him, but Tim does not always have the best discernment on fashion.) Thank goodness for shopping filters. They save me so much time when I need to find a shoe in exactly the color, size, and heel I want.

Without filters, I add things to my cart that I don't really need. You know, the "other" pair of shoes that are shiny and trendy, that would work so well with the dress I wear whenever the stars have aligned and I've had time to shave my legs. (Those impulse shoes typically sit in my closet, neglected in their unopened boxes.) The filters save me time and direct me toward what I *actually* need.

Finding lasting friendships can feel even more overwhelming and exhausting than online shopping. Not because the women aren't out there but because we may not have the right filters on in our search—or we may not use filters at all.

Yep, that's right: Just like appropriate filters keep you from ending up with a mustard-colored blouse two sizes too small, filters can help you discern which friendships are the right fit.

Of all the women in our community, how do we know whom to invest our time and energy into? Are we so overwhelmed by choices that we forget what we are looking for in a friend? Or do we give up before we even start?

We also can't promise to be best friends with each person we meet, but without the right filter, we may end up with too many numbers in our phones and neglect the women who thought we were serious about becoming friends. The guilt surrounding neglected friends is real. Using our friendship filters wisely helps us avoid having to backtrack and confess we may have been a bit too eager.

I bounced from friend to friend in college with no clue how to identify a true friend. In many scenarios, I gravitated toward the "popular" kids because they were well-known on campus (which I thought meant they would be cool people to befriend); they were usually the ones who didn't respond to my text the next day. Other times, I cancelled plans last minute with my roommate to go get froyo with girls from class because I didn't want to miss out on the opportunity to spend time with them. This wasn't a bad choice, but it reflected poorly on my ability to be a faithful friend to my roommate. My lack of intentionality around pursuing friends seemed harmless, but years went by, and I still felt disconnected and a bit lost. What *was* a friend? Who was I as a friend to others?

Finding true friends doesn't always happen smoothly, but it is possible to create habits that help you refine your search. I've discovered that it is really a threefold process:

1. Know yourself. (Evaluate your strengths and weaknesses as a friend.)
2. Know your friendship needs. (What type of friend are you looking for?)
3. Use what you've learned to search for women who align with your friendship style and values.

As the proverb says, "The righteous choose their friends carefully."[1] Deep friendships grow out of shared values, which means that intentional friendship filters are essential. Let's be wise and purposeful in how we find our friends.

KNOW YOURSELF

When I moved to Denver, I wanted to be more thoughtful about finding friends. I didn't have twelve years of grade school to build besties. I was juggling multiple priorities as a young adult in a new city. My strategy for finding godly friends was going to look different than it had in high school or college. And my first filter needed to be myself.

We often attract the type of friends we are most like—so being a quality friend is of the utmost importance. I am not saying we need to all be the same, but we can value the same things. Shopping filters don't always show us the exact item, but they do match our preferences for a certain style. In the same way, don't expect your friendship filters to locate potential friends who are exactly like you, but use them to understand what you will or won't settle for in friendship.

Thankfully, we don't need to start our search from scratch. The Bible provides the best filters for what healthy, lasting friendships look like. It even takes into account the person we are becoming in Jesus:

- *Do I serve others—without expecting anything in return?*

  "Greater love has no one than this, that someone lay down his life for his friends." (John 15:13)

- *Does our conversation leave us both refreshed?*

  "The sweetness of a friend comes from [her] earnest counsel." (Proverbs 27:9)

- *Do I stand by my friends during the good, the bad, and the mundane parts of life?*

  "A man of many companions may come to ruin, but there is a friend who sticks closer than a brother." (Proverbs 18:24)

- *Am I trustworthy? Do I offer wise advice when asked, or do I volunteer opinions when they're not wanted? Do I seek advice from trusted friends and mentors to help me grow?*

  "Plans fail for lack of counsel, but with many advisers they succeed." (Proverbs 15:22)

- *Am I intentionally growing in my faith so I may better sharpen my friends in theirs?*

  "Iron sharpens iron, and one [woman] sharpens another." (Proverbs 27:17)

- *Do I use my words to lift others up?*

  "Let no corrupting talk come out of your mouths, but only such as is good for building up, as fits the occasion, that it may give grace to those who hear." (Ephesians 4:29)

- *Do I respect myself and others?*

  "As you wish that others would do to you, do so to them." (Luke 6:31)

- *Do I see my friends as a gift, not something to treat carelessly?*

  "Behold, how good and pleasant it is when [sisters] dwell together in unity!" (Psalm 133:1)

- *Even when we disagree, do I seek to understand and listen instead of arguing to be right?*

  "A friend loves at all times, and a [sister] is born for adversity." (Proverbs 17:17)

- *Do I walk with humility?*

  "Do nothing from selfish ambition or conceit, but in humility count others more significant than yourselves. Let each of you look not only to [her] own interests, but also to the interests of others." (Philippians 2:3-4)

- *Am I secure in Christ's love, giving love away without threat to my personal worth?*

  "We love because he first loved us." (1 John 4:19)

Maybe you are reading these character qualities and finding yourself sinking deeper and deeper into your chair.

What about that thing I said a few years back that was meant to be hurtful and mean?

41

What about the time I left someone out on purpose?

What about yesterday when I was feeling too lazy to answer a friend's text?

I get it. I do.

We all mess up. I mess up!

Applying wise friendship filters to ourselves first helps us enter relationships with others from a place of humility and wisdom. As Christians, we do not rely on our own strength to produce the fruit of the Spirit and other Jesus-like qualities listed above. We are all growing, and there is room for us to grow in these areas of being a friend too.

KNOW YOUR NEEDS

Okay, okay—so a list is nice and all, but sometimes we have some real, tangible friendship needs. My social connections in Denver consisted of one person I knew from my hometown (whom I barely kept in contact with). Meeting lots of people was a priority. Finding friends was not going to happen in a middle-age knitting club or in a packed bar downtown. A busy bar scene was not my vibe, and as much as I value wiser, older women in my circle, I needed some friends who would know my references to the movie *Clueless*.

So, on my Denver friendship search, I decided to join a younger church, with folks mostly in their twenties and thirties, so I had the best possible chance of connecting with like-minded women. I had grown up attending a multigenerational church, so I had some guilt about passing up on the richness of a more diverse community. But for this season, I needed some friends in my life ASAP—so I found a healthy church I could invest in and set myself up to meet friends quickly.

Not only was I looking for the qualities above but I was also looking for women who were able to reciprocate time with me. My flexible student schedule made it easier for me to be present with others, but if I didn't get the sense that someone was willing to make the extra effort, then I knew that friendship was not going to work. No one can sustain a one-sided friendship.

I look back with fondness at this time because many of my friends were new to Denver—we found each other simply out of a need to get connected. Since then, all these friends have moved away and created new friend groups in their new cities, but at the time, we made up a community we all desperately needed.

I get a bit teary-eyed at these lyrics from the musical *Wicked*:

> *Who can say if I've been changed for the better?*
> *But because I knew you, I have been changed for good.*[2]

That song puts words to what I feel about these first Denver friends. They didn't end up being lifelong friends, but those two years we had together changed me for good. As you are looking for friends, don't get too caught up in the ones that didn't last forever (though some may). God knows what He is doing; His timing is perfect. He brings friends into your life to get you through things and vice versa. Remember that one acquaintance from my hometown I mentioned earlier? She took me to dinner after I had moved to town; we shared only an hour together, but making time to connect recharged me in a way I needed to get through the difficult transition. We didn't see each other after that, though not on purpose. But I have not forgotten that divine appointment, which gave me the energy to fall in love with Denver and find my place among my current community. There's no shame (and no expectation) in not making each connection point into a forever friend. Instead we can thank Jesus for the good these women brought into our lives when we needed them the most.

These days, I am reevaluating my friendship needs all over again. There may never be a feeling of *I made it* when it comes to finding and making friends. People will move, friendships will end, or sometimes we simply grow apart and loneliness seeps back in. Your friendship *needs* will grow and change, which does not indicate you are having a friendship identity crisis; it just means *you* are growing and changing. There is freedom when we receive and release friends based on our life stage and the things we need in that stage.

USE WHAT YOU'VE LEARNED

Friendship filters gave me clarity as I pursued new relationships. I decided to not take any chances when I saw a person I admired, respected, and wanted to get to know better. I wouldn't play "hard to get" in friendship, pretending I only sort of wanted to be friends. Instead, I was honest and clear, asking them if they would like to be real friends—the kind of friends who would walk through the different transitions in life with me.

That new-to-Denver season of my life was important for practicing healthy friendship practices. Without knowing it, I built the foundation for my current season of married life with three kids and a job. Using filters has given me such clarity, like when I met my good friend Rachel.

In 2018, I met Rachel at a women's writing event I hosted in Denver. We met and had friendly chat but nothing more. When we ran across each other's paths a second time, the way she intently listened after asking a thoughtful question really stood out. She was genuine, and she loved Jesus with her whole heart. She was great at initiating hangouts. I hadn't even really decided if I wanted to pursue the friendship when she asked to go on walks and invited my son, Hunter, over to meet chickens she was house-sitting. (Yes, chickens! Clearly this girl was too cool for me.)

The real kicker is when she offered to watch my kids for free because she was so passionate about helping me find time to write this book. I mean, how could you not want a friend like that in your life? The Lord opened my eyes to see the potential for a lasting friendship with Rachel. Our conversations were filled with reflections on how the gospel influences our marriage, jobs, communities, and neighborhoods. This meaningful time moved us from acquaintances to writing buddies—and eventually to committed friends.

She freely offered up her most precious gift, her time. She never said, "Let's be best friends for life," but her actions communicated, "Let's invest in each other."

As soon as we started to become good friends, I found out she was moving back to her hometown in Arkansas. In full disclosure, I had two conflicting thoughts:

1. *Close this door now. She's leaving, and it's time to shift my priorities to friends who are sticking around.*

2. *I think this friendship has the foundation to last despite the distance. I am going to continue to invest in her and our relationship as much as I can before she leaves.*

Thankfully I listened to the latter. We had six weeks before her big move, so we planned to see each other multiple times each of these weeks. As I write this, she has been away from Denver for years now, and we have found creative ways to keep our friendship strong. We use a social-media app, Marco Polo, to stay in touch regularly. We pray for one another, talk about the books we're reading, and discuss how we wish we danced as well as every contestant on *World of Dance.*

When Rachel and her husband came back to visit Denver the fall after they moved, they needed a place to stay for a week, and we agreed to host them. Our time together in person enriched and deepened the friendship we had developed over the phone. We still make trips to visit each other to this day. While a phone conversation is a nice substitute, nothing compares to quality girl time, sitting on the couch eating a giant bowl of popcorn, in person.

After years of having good friends, flaky friends, and friends for a certain season, I've found it easier and easier to identify what could become a meaningful friendship.

Intentionality and experience using my filters helps me more readily see the potential in a lasting friend—one that can even span states.

Here are some ways I notice someone who could be a lasting friend:

- **A lasting friend keeps the circle open.** A woman who always has room for one more friend demonstrates God's welcoming nature. No one wants to jump through hoops to receive the approval of other women. A lasting friend always invites people into the conversation.

- **A lasting friend values and protects her friend time.** She knows growth happens when she consistently tends to the people in her life. Her love is expressed in shared experiences and building an unshakeable bond together.

- **A lasting friend celebrates those around her.** She knows how to celebrate others without feeling threatened. Her identity is in Christ, so she doesn't fear another woman being better at something than she is or having something that she doesn't. She finds authentic joy for her friends' successes and good news.

- **A lasting friend shows grace.** No friend should have to walk on eggshells every time they make a mistake. A lasting friend communicates grace through her actions *and* her words, so her friends never have to wonder or worry where they stand when the friendship hits a bump!

- **A lasting friend knows her words can tear down or build up others.** She knows words hold weight, so she thinks before she speaks. If she says something out of spite, bitterness, or jealousy, she is the first to acknowledge what she did and ask for forgiveness. She uses her words to build her friends up, knowing that those thoughtful encouragements will take root and blossom in her friends' lives.

- **A lasting friend sows trust.** She is capable of deep conversation and trustworthy, holding intimate knowledge close to her heart. She keeps her promises and shows up when she says she will. Not only is she a good listener but she's also humbled enough to share her own struggles and needs.

- **A lasting friend points others to Jesus.** A woman who sharpens the faith of her friends is one to be valued! She asks hard questions; she knows God and His Word; she loves well. She is a friend of God, and she passes on that joy and love to the people around her.

WHEN A FRIENDSHIP ISN'T RECIPROCATED

You've put yourself out there, gone to the girls' nights and the Bible studies, and you are still struggling to make a friendship connection. You are giving your best and women aren't reciprocating the efforts. This friendship thing can be so tricky!

As a classic initiator, I deeply feel the pain of someone not reciprocating my efforts. I have had many budding friendships meet their end when friends reschedule over and over, stop responding to texts, or just disappear. You may also have heard this disappearing act as "ghosting."

In her book *Give It a Rest*, friendship coach Danielle Bayard Jackson talks about the damaging effects of our cut-off culture:

> Cut-off culture refers to the increasingly accepted practice of completely ending communication with someone without warning or explanation. . . .
> . . . We choose to ghost other women when we decide that moving forward would be too hard.[3]

Silent treatment is, in my experience, the most common response in friendships when things have stalled. Many of us are left to wonder: *Was I not worthy of her time? Was I not an interesting enough person to invest in?* Friendship ghosting has made me doubt my worth many times. There is also the potential for new friendships to stall due to an unexpected conflict early in the friendship. Instead of addressing the issue, the stonewalling lasts a few months until the conflict has been "forgotten," or it ends a friendship altogether. Being "cut- off" is more painful than a difficult conversation would have been. This sort of ghosting has made me second-guess all my friendships (*Does she really like me, or will she disappear without any explanation too?*).

I had my first real friendship ghosting situation in my mid-twenties. Sure, I had already experienced plenty of mutual partings due to "growing apart." But in this new friendship, a relationship I thought was healthy and fine did a complete 180-degree turn. My friend kept putting off my invitations to hang out, then ignored my calls, and finally sent me a text saying, "Wish you the best." I had done something that hurt her feelings through a misunderstood text message, but her refusal to talk through things and reconcile was just as painful. I had enjoyed this friendship so much and invested a lot of time, and I still really liked this girl despite her callous behavior.

The friendship was clearly over, but without an actual, clear conversation, the vague conclusion was difficult to process. I spent many nights crying into my pillow. I called the friend to ask if we could please speak in person, but it wasn't until many months later when I ran into her at a party that we had an opportunity to talk. We apologized for how we handled the situation and walked away with some peace. We respected what our friendship had been and would have genuine friendliness when we ran across each other in the future, but it was unlikely we would reestablish a friendship.

This may seem like a sad ending to the story, but I discovered that ultimately it was a rich opportunity to see God's reconciliation at work. I was prayerful in this time, asking God to give me humility to hear where I fell short and to help me forgive my friend's mistakes. I trusted God to work in both of our hearts even though we weren't talking. I walked away from our last conversation with so much peace and praise, despite the outcome, because I knew God was part of it all. I had done my best to respect myself and my friend and honor God through the experience.

When we're tempted to silently withdraw instead of addressing a friendship issue, here are some thoughts from God's Word to comfort us:

If your [sister] sins against you, go and tell
[her her] fault, between you and [her] alone.
If [she] listens to you, you have gained your
[sister].

MATTHEW 18:15

Repay no one evil for evil, but give thought to do
what is honorable in the sight of all. If possible, so
far as it depends on you, live peaceably with all.

ROMANS 12:17-18

Whether you are the one backing out of a friendship or
you feel that a friend has stopped putting in the effort, my
best advice is to *talk about it*. Even if the reason for your with-
drawal is as innocent as being too busy for her, sometimes
communicating your level of commitment to the friendship is better than not communicating about it at all. The
ghosting culture has to stop. It is unbiblical and damaging.
Instead, with humility, approach your friend and do everything you can to make peace with her. At that point it is on
her to respond in truth and love. If she doesn't, she will need
to work that out with God, not you. You have done everything you can, and that alone will provide you the peace to
begin your friend search again.

YOU'VE GOT A FRIEND IN ME

Using your search filters regularly will increase your ability to discover how you best approach making new friends. The process for filtering friends may seem slow, but once you've decided on the potential friends to pursue, your confidence will move your friendships toward depth and meaning much faster. Hello, future friends everywhere!

Friendship Tip: As you filter friends for yourself, you'll also get good at identifying potential friends for others. Maybe you have a full plate of friends, or maybe you meet someone who would be a great friend for someone you know. Connect them! I love doing this. When a new girl joins our small group or a friend from college moves to town, I like to connect them with someone who shares the same friendship qualities. What a gift to set up an opportunity for them to meet and to witness them create a meaningful relationship.

FRIENDSHIP PEP TALK:

Find Your People

Find your people;
pursue them on purpose.

3

DIY FRIENDSHIP

Building the Friendship You Want

"I can do this," I whisper to myself as I step onto the porch of my friend's home.

I have felt this way before: paralyzed by social fear, coaching myself to enter the laughter and conversation already happening inside. The warm light shines down through the window, and even though I know rich life waits inside this home, a small voice tells me it would be better, safer to leave right now.

Just hours ago, I was excited about being part of a girls' night. I had clicked play on my "girl time" playlist (consisting of "Girls Just Want to Have Fun" and anything by Taylor Swift). But now I stand paralyzed outside while the doubt floods in. *What if I don't see any familiar faces? What if no one talks to me? Are my jeans and blouse too dressy? Everyone wears cute athleisure in Colorado—should I have stuck with cute athleisure?*

I run through different scenarios that might lessen the awkwardness I'll feel when I walk in the door. Perhaps I could play wingwoman to the host and offer to help in any way I can. I can't feel left out if I have a job to do, right? Or maybe if I just keep my mouth full of chips, no one will feel like they have to start a conversation with me.

Or should I just turn around and go home? I mean, it's been a long day. I *am* kind of tired. Starting new conversations sounds exhausting. My bed sounds so nice. I can just pick up some food on the way home.

Welp, that's that. I have talked myself out of another opportunity to connect with friends because of a little internal nudge to stay in my comfort zone.

Sometimes making new friends or connecting with old ones just feels like too much effort. Even after you have done the hard work of filtering some godly friends, the actual work of building on those initial invites is challenging.

This anxiety about connecting with another human being

isn't just limited to group gatherings, either! Maybe you're just meeting for coffee with a new person you met at church. Or going on a run with a friend from the gym. Every new interaction brings risk.

We come to this friendship threshold often, wanting to step into a relationship full of potential but weighed down with a variety of fears. Fears like . . .

- *How much investment will this friendship take?*
- *What happens when I show my true colors?*
- *What if I don't fit in with her other friends?*
- *What if she doesn't care as much about the friendship as I do?*

Digging into new friendship can be daunting. Uncertainty about whether people will like us for who we are (once we finally show our true colors) is intimidating. Rejection is painful; and we are anxious when a social interaction doesn't go the way we planned. (Sometimes I leave a gathering and think: *That was not my best work.*) Instead of acknowledging our fears, we *pretend* friendship doesn't matter all that much to us. If we don't make a big fuss over the details, we won't get hurt.

But meaningful friendships require active and intentional

pursuit. No one is going to go out there and create friendships for us. As nice as it would be for someone to hand-select our perfect best friend, complete with years of memories and dozens of shared interests, that's not how it works.

So, what does it look like to be proactive about our friendships? Well, the work of building new relationships is a bit like a DIY project—and we already know the first two steps:

1. Have the right tools (invest in your friendship with Jesus).
2. Do the research and know the level of effort the project will require (use your friendship filters).

And lastly?

3. Do the actual work. (Why start someday when you can start today?)

I know what you're thinking. A lot of us hear "DIY" and immediately feel out of our depth. So before we dive too deeply into our fears around *that*, let me tell you about my relationship with DIY *anything*.

For my twenty-eighth birthday party, I came up with what seemed like the perfect project to do with my friends:

dyeing kitchen towels. I scrolled through Pinterest, looking for the perfect DIY hand-dyed ombré towel instructions; I read a few blogs; then I thought, *I get the gist. I can give this a try.* Famous last words.

My lack of attention to detail renders most of my DIY projects "Pinterest fails." *But,* I told myself, *things will be different this time.* I could not possibly fail with these ombré kitchen towels.

So, naturally, I took some shortcuts and ended up with a towel that was not a beautiful ombré of various shades of pink but just pink . . . all over. My party guests were asking all sorts of questions about why their towels didn't look like the picture inspiration I showed them. Whoops. Thankfully, they all appreciated having a new towel to take home, even if it didn't make the cute design we all hoped for.

Later, like a complete newb, I washed the pink towel with all my other dishtowels. Now every towel in the kitchen is tinted pink.

Consider this an ode to all the ideas and recipes we have pinned but never tried or tried and failed at miserably (RIP "Blackberry Cucumber Caprese Skewers" and "Effortless Homemade Valentine's Day Doughnut Wall for Kids").

All the crafts and goodies *look* great, but attention to detail, confidence, skills, and time often hold us back from doing a DIY project well. Tim, my champion for *buying* home decor over crafting it, has gently encouraged me to pause all my DIY projects until I know what I am doing before I start *and* promise to do it diligently.

This applies to friendship too! We've got to understand our investment in this big endeavor so we can confidently pursue friendship without giving up, getting frustrated, or pouring a bottle of glitter on the less-than-perfect parts of friendship to make it look prettier (okay, so that one just applies to Pinterest fails).

UNDERSTAND THE COMMITMENT

Wishful thinking won't turn a friendship into what you hope or dream it will look like. When you're making or maintaining friends, you need to know what you're committing to so the obstacles don't deter you from the big picture—sharing life together.

Maybe you've already experienced this: giving up when schedules become too challenging to coordinate, getting tired of listening to their latest breakup story, or dealing with frustration when their kids constantly interrupt your conversations. Obstacles are part of any relationship. What matters is what we do with them.

It's like the trite saying, "You get what you put in." When

I'm coaching other women about the friend-making process, I often recommend they commit to a certain time frame for building the friendship before they can officially say, "This isn't going anywhere." Give it three to six months of consistently showing up and being present. Then you can't use the excuse that a friendship "just didn't work out." If you give the friendship your best effort and it still doesn't work out, then you know you at least gave the other person multiple opportunities to develop a lasting friendship.

When I talked myself out of girls' night, I wasn't quite committed to my friend-making process—the fact that I actually have to put myself out there to know people and let them know me. I often get stuck prejudging a person or a situation. As I anxiously wonder whether a person will like me, I self-protect by telling myself, *They just aren't my people* or *They probably won't be very inclusive*. But this holds me back from real connection with potential friends.

Over time, I've learned that I should never judge a potential friend based solely on my first impression of them because I am oftentimes wrong about those initial greetings. Also, I wouldn't want people to judge me as a new friend based off how outgoing or friendly I was feeling that day. Choosing to commit to a new friend gives people the benefit of the doubt for "off" days and social nervousness. Agreeing to see a new friendship through the awkward beginning stages leaves things open for a real friendship to take shape.

ENGAGE IN THE PROCESS

We can't be surprised when we find ourselves needing to make new friends at age twenty-one, thirty-five, fifty, or even seventy. As friendship expert Shasta Nelson notes, "We can do everything right to build up friendships and still find ourselves in a place where we have to do it again. Life shifts. Our needs shift. Our friendships shift."[1] We are always in the business of being a friend. And so, to participate in this lifelong pursuit of friendship, we need to *engage* with the process of making and being a friend.

When I began to make community in Denver, I knew a nice first conversation wasn't enough to create a friendship. I snagged phone numbers, scheduled walks in the park, and set up picnic dinners. I tried to remember birthdays and made sure to send snail mail to potential friends as we got to know one another. I knew there had to be more to friendship than just hoping women would knock on my door, begging to be my bestie. I needed to make those first moves myself if I wanted to create a meaningful community. I learned to pursue new friends in the same way I would want to be pursued—which included helping watch their kids, knowing their favorite coffee drink, and remembering the big and little moments of their lives. Some may say, "Well, you are just naturally friendly or extroverted." Sometimes I am. But it's really Jesus who helps us in the do-it-yourself stages of friendship.

Jesus' love compels us to do the unthinkable, awkward parts of initiating friendship—"And he died for all, that those who live should no longer live for themselves but for him who died for them and was raised again."[2] We don't live for ourselves any longer. We live for Jesus and have confidence in what Jesus has done for us *and*

the woman sitting across the table,

the one next to our cubicle,

the giggling group of girls inside,

the friend waiting for our text response.

Remembering that Jesus has compassion for every woman—because we are all looking to be loved and accepted and known—makes engaging in friend-making less about how we look and more about sharing the love of Jesus with others. We can lay down our insecurities around committing to and engaging in new friendships because our intentions are motivated by serving others versus serving ourselves. Still, I won't downplay how uncomfortable it can be to follow up with a new friend, hoping she feels the same! Yet, when the relationship feels right, someone will be honored by your initiative to bring her into the folds of friendship just like Jesus did for us.

Engaging with new friends won't always go the way you want. But remember: Your personal worth is not on the chopping block every time you reach out to another person. When you feel rejected, God may be protecting you from a friend who would have not valued you or your time. My friend Kelsey always says, "Rejection is God's protection." I carry that saying with me often in these tense friend-making moments. I can step out trusting God is orchestrating my steps and relationships.

Friendship Tip: Introverts, are you totally freaking out on me? Initiating time with other people may be the last thing you are interested in, but that doesn't mean you want to miss out on the fun of making new friends, either. Make sure you think ahead when friend plans come up. Build in time to recharge before and after the friend date. Also, don't be pressured to approach friendship the same way an extroverted person may approach it. Stay true to who you are, and find friend settings where you feel most comfortable to open up and shine.

STATE YOUR INTENTIONS

A new friend and I were sitting at a downtown bar in Denver, and I knew it was time to be direct about my desire for a deeper friendship. At the time I had a myriad of acquaintances from grad school or church, but I still didn't have many dependable friendships. I wanted a sister-in-Christ who would be the mac to my cheese, the peanut butter to my jelly . . . you get the idea. I wanted a friend who "sticks closer than a brother."[3]

So I gathered my courage and told her:

"I'd really like it if we could become close friends."

The music was loud, and I wasn't sure she heard me, so I said it again: "I want this to be a lifelong, real friendship. I want to hold each other accountable. Meet regularly. I want to come to a place where we can text each other about our embarrassing moments and irrational fears. I want to talk about Scripture with you. I want to get to a point where we would call one another best friends."

That time she heard me. I tugged on my sweater uncomfortably and pushed the food around on my plate as I waited to hear what she would say.

There is a moment in female friendships when we are ready for the next step. We've leaned into our relationship with Jesus and are working on our negative thought patterns, we've used our filters, and we've determined the kind of friend we want to pursue—but now it's time to name our hopes for the friendship out loud, to see if the other person is up for sharing that goal. It's time to see the friendship through.

As I sat with my friend and shared how I would define a real friendship, I slowly watched her face go from *Did I just hear you correctly?* to lighting up with a genuine smile. She said she was interested in an intentional friendship too. We made a plan to see each other at least once a month. When we'd get together, we would always schedule the next month's hangout so we wouldn't allow busy schedules to get in the way of getting to know each other.

Now, I haven't had this type of conversation thirty times, or even five. Sometimes friendships happen naturally—when we have a weekly Bible study together, work on the same project at school, or enjoy the same takeout for lunch on Fridays. But there have been moments when I felt the Lord leading me to be direct with a friend, to lead the way in naming our shared desire for deeper connection.

Think about one or two women you really enjoy spending time with. What would it look like to be direct with them about your hopes for your friendship, to get to the real richness of friendship by letting them know you are committed to be a dependable friend to them? Share your intentions and ask for what you want in your friendship.

You want someone to pray with you every Tuesday morning? Ask her.

You want to be closer to your roommate? Accept her invitation to watch a movie together.

You want married couple friends from the neighborhood? Invite them to a monthly dinner party.

Here is your opportunity to stick to a DIY project—your very own pursuit of your people!

Expect some dings and dents along the way—that's just how relationships go. We all have different capacities for creating community, so there isn't one-size-fits-all when it comes to do-it-yourself friendship. Even if your first friendship attempts aren't perfect, they are still steps forward. That little-by-little work gets us to our vision for the friendship we "pinned" so many years ago.

No matter how many Pinterest fails we have in *other* areas of our lives, we're all capable of developing rich friendships. No one is going to do it for you—but no one can do it quite like you, either.

FRIEND-DATE IDEA:

Cake Day

Building community, one forkful of cake at a time!

We all need excuses to spend time together. My community uses Cake Day as a monthly rhythm to connect with friends. It's simple. It's meaningful. It's cake!

How to host your own Cake Day:

1. Pick a day every month to celebrate Cake Day.

2. It doesn't matter what type of cake is used. You can change it up every month or eat red velvet twelve times—wherever your baking experience leads you.

3. Place the number of candles on the cake that coordinates with the month you're celebrating (one for January, two for February, etc.).

4. Provide paper flags and ask your guests to write down
   one thing God has done in their life in the last month.
   (If your guests wouldn't be comfortable with that
   prompt, you can always ask: What are you grateful for
   from the last month?) Each person shares their God-
   win and places their flag in the cake.

5. Light your candles, turn off the lights, and sing the
   Cake Day song. We have made up our own tune in
   my community, so feel free to go where the Spirit
   leads with the notes. Just make sure you've practiced
   it a few times as a group:

   Cake Day. Cakeus Diem.
   Oo loo loo. Oo la la.
   Let's eat cake!
   (one clap)

6. Everyone can blow out the candles, or
   you can designate a special someone.

7. Finally, *eat* the cake—BUT HOLD ON . . . *no*
   plates are allowed. Only utensils. Everyone digs
   into the cake for as many bites as they please.

* *If someone in your group is gluten-free, get them a mini gluten-free dessert so they don't feel left out.*
** *If you feel a cold coming on, take the ceremonious first bite and then put some cake for yourself on a plate, so no germs are spread.*

The power of Cake Day is that it gives everyone a shared experience—and anyone, at any age, can participate. You may have entered as strangers, but now you have a common experience to laugh about later. Cake Day breaks down the awkward barriers of first hellos and ushers in the potential for real friendship.

4

NEVER TOO BUSY

Knocking Down the Barrier of Time

Recently I surveyed women on Instagram, asking them to identify their biggest struggle in friendship. There were a few things, like "Trying to find friends in a new city" and "Healing from a friendship breakup." But most of the responses were: "I'm too busy!" Some said they were busy in the mom phase. Some just wished their calendars aligned more with that of their friends. Others felt like there was not enough time juggling work and personal priorities. And it's true—navigating life is complicated, and being a good friend on top of everything else is overwhelming. But if we long to build true friendship, we've got to acknowledge that one of our biggest barriers is not being busy. It's *believing* that we are too busy for our friends or that our friends are too busy for us.

One of the most impactful ways to create lasting friendship? Shared time.

See the disparity?

We want quality gal pals, but we believe there is just no time to create those kinds of friendship. So we wait for our schedules to slow down, which . . . doesn't usually happen. Whenever I have attempted to grow a friendship based off "the next time we're free," that was a *big*, flashing sign that the friendship wouldn't get off the ground.

Constancy is a key ingredient for the recipe to great friendship. Without it, friendships grow stale. A fragmented relationship is incapable of nourishing anyone.

So, why is being consistent in our friendships so challenging?

Yes, our time and our schedules create issues—but our hearts are the starting point when we are too busy for friends.

Today's culture often treats a friend as "someone who meets your needs or fits into your schedule—a matter of convenience."[1] We approach our friendships with the hope that they will meet our demands and make life easier and more pleasant for us. So, when scheduling time together complicates our calendars, we can feel the tension that is a real part of trying to manage a friendship.

Another struggle we face? We all have our own perceptions of "busy," which means we end up struggling to work with different friends' capacity for shared time.

In Denver, some people deem "busy" as attending every summer concert at the Red Rocks venue.

Others find a new dating relationship hard to manage.

Some people (like me) are new moms, sacrificing a girls' night because the kids need to get to bed on time.

Wherever you land, "busy" can make us feel helpless in tending to our friendships.

When we were expecting our first kid, Hunter, I mourned a lot of the changes that would take place once I was a mom. One of the things I mourned the most was my friend time. I wasn't sure what my capacity would be for friendship. I had seen other women abandon relationships when they became mothers, and that really frightened me. It wasn't my personality to give up on my friends, but seasoned mothers made it seem like the norm. My fear of the future "busy" to come gave me the push to make a plan.

The baby came, and unforeseen scheduling challenges like nursing and nap times came with him. (Babies always seem to know when you make plans with friends—they act up right when you're ready to go out and do something.) As hard as I tried to manage my friendships at the same pace I had before kids, life was just different. My concept of busy was different, which is fine. You may experience newness in your life in different ways. To each of us, the changes can be overwhelming—emotionally, physically, mentally, et cetera. We don't have to feel guilty about our pace of life changing. We just need to figure out what friendship in our new normal looks like.

But I fought against the new normal constantly. I had yet to submit to my new role as a mother; I wanted to fit my old routine into my new routine. You don't know what you don't know as you enter new things, and instead of being able to communicate about it, I just pretended nothing was different for me.

So, four days into being a new parent, I had the brilliant idea to host an Olympic watch party at our house. I was still trying to figure out the whole nursing cover . . . and well, nursing in general. As I sat on the couch and Hunter fussed, I stressed about not making our single guy friends uncomfortable. Excusing myself to go attempt a feeding in the nursery, I tried to hold back tears. After I put him in his crib, I brushed back tears and went back into the party as if everything was as it had been months before—no limits to my ability to be present with friends. My new reality was unavoidable, and for the first time as a young adult, I needed to set boundaries for myself and my friends to protect my newly growing family.

Still, my new lack of availability was a constant source of anxiety for me. Were my friends frustrated that I couldn't pack for an overnight camping trip with a two-month-old? I had to leave dinner parties early because Hunter needed to eat before he went to bed. Did my friends assume I cared less about them for ducking out before the cake? At a time when I needed to connect with friends more than ever, I felt pulled in a lot of directions. I was so insecure adding a baby to the mix, when the trouble I assumed a little one would cause was mostly in my head. Was it really that difficult, or was I just unwilling to shift my priorities to make sure genuine connection was still happening despite the new changes?

At the same time, my friends looked at me and thought, *She has so much going on as a new mom. She is probably too busy to spend time with me.* The invitations stopped coming because they were afraid to put me in a tough position. We both wanted to connect but assumed that busyness was too big of a barrier for us to find time for each other.

When we think we are too busy for friends or that they

are too busy for us, we aren't fighting our schedule. We are fighting our *priorities*. We step back because we are uncertain of what it would look like if we decided "busy" could no longer be our excuse for uncharted friend territory.

You've got to decide if making time for friendships is a priority for you. Is it worth it?

TIME AND FRIENDSHIP

A recent study at the University of Kansas uncovered how many hours it would take to make a "close" friend—someone you would call your best friend. You know, the kind of friend you can share everything with, like when you find your first gray hair (and they immediately assure you that you are still a goddess).

Here is what they found: From the moment you meet someone, it takes fifty hours of social interaction to get to the point where you're able to call them an acquaintance.[2] This includes the conversation about your family around the conference table, the walk you take with your neighbor, or the logistics of working on a project with a girl in your class. After fifty hours of "How are you?" and "What's your favorite show?" you now have a friendly face you can seek out in social situations.

Going from being acquaintances to being good friends

requires an additional forty hours of social interactions. This means you need to make space for *ninety total hours* of social time to build a friendship.

FROM STRANGERS TO ACQUAINTANCES

0
hours

strangers

90
hours

friends

How are we expected to find ninety hours in our schedule to make a new friend? That sounds almost impossible to many adults.

That's why we reminisce fondly about high-school or college friends. We spent several days together a week, several hours a day, studying together, hanging out, talking. Those ninety hours happened fast.

My childhood best friend and I shared the same class schedule and the same extracurriculars, and we were even involved in all the same church activities. We looked nothing alike, but I would have considered us twins. We also had some strange best-friend telepathy where we would choose to wear the same shirt or headband on the same day. In the morning, we would text each other, "Don't wear your yellow shirt today" just so we wouldn't come to school matching (though I wouldn't have hated it if we did). During our school years, social time is automatically built into our schedules.

But once you're past those seasons of life, finding friend time requires intentional work.

Oh, and by the way, guess how long that study said it takes for two strangers to become best friends?

Two hundred hours of social time.

Two hundred! That may be more than two years' worth of free time I have for one friend among working, sleeping, juggling date nights, navigating kid's activities, hosting small group, and making three meals a day for five people. It's too much!

Friendship feels like too much.

Right?

Wrong.

Busyness is the enemy's disguise to keep us from starting a new friendship or growing a current one. He tells us friendship is too costly.

But, as a lifelong friendship builder and a busy woman, I can honestly say this: Making an intentional decision to prioritize friendship a little at a time does eventually add up to something great. You don't need to log the exact numbers this study suggests, but you also can't build a friendship on hopes and "Let's get together soon."

Do you believe your life is less about your to-do list and more about ministering to your people?

Do you believe God values your friendships?

Do you value your friendships as much as He does?

LAY DOWN YOUR AGENDA

As I reconciled my desire for friendship at the cost of my sanity and the balance of being a good friend, I came upon this Bible passage over and over:

> This is my commandment, that you love one
> another as I have loved you. Greater love has no
> one than this, that someone lay down his life for
> his friends.
>
> JOHN 15:12-13

Jesus' love is sacrificial. Our lives were never too costly for Him. He chose to die so we could be saved and reconciled back into a healthy relationship with Him. To Jesus, restoring friendship with us was worth the sacrifice.

Loving my community the way Jesus loves me means

laying aside my agenda for the sake of loving my friends the way Jesus does. My friends need to know that our friendship is not too costly. And thankfully, God's love gives us the genuine strength and joy to make time for them.

We are less threatened by our busy schedules when we are overwhelmed by God's love.

But what does "lay down our lives" mean? Do I need to jump in front of a bullet for my girlfriends? Do I need to choose them over something I need to do for my health or family?

Sacrificial love does not put us at jeopardy. Our friendships are not healthy or fulfilling if we always play the part of a martyr. We don't need to die for our friends or abandon our other relational priorities. But one way of laying our lives down for our friends is making the necessary sacrifices to love them more than we love our busy schedule. We can choose people over projects or personal comfort.

But I also want to admit that the sacrificial way we learn to love our friends isn't something any of us do perfectly or consistently. God's love is perfect, but we are far from reflecting that love in the same way. I still have selfish thoughts and desires when a friend asks me to do something I don't want to do—whether it's as simple as going on a walk when I just want to watch TV or as complicated as helping them move on a Saturday when I have family time scheduled. We can't look at Jesus' sacrifice and assume that He skipped and sang His way down the difficult and violent path it took to save the world. He was human, after all. Jesus felt deeply the sacrifice of the cross. He even prayed and asked God to take away the burden before Him. Sacrifice isn't easy just because it's done for the sake of others. But Jesus' humility shows us the way through our resistance to sacrificing for our friends: "Yet not my will, but yours be done"[3]—a prayer we can all say when we find ourselves stuck in the lie of *I'm too busy to be a friend.*

God's plan for reconciling relationships was *surrender* and *sacrifice.* Jesus, then, is our example of a perfect friend. We are commissioned to do the same: surrender our priorities to God's direction and offer sacrificial love through our actions.

Maybe we're prioritizing our job, our exercise class, or our dating life over friendship. Those aren't necessarily bad things to spend your time and energy on—but when a friend needs you, can you sacrifice your time to be an agent of love?

SHIFTING PRIORITIES

I am a recovering task addict. In my early college years, I would write out my daily schedule minute-by-minute, including when I would use the bathroom and for how long

(I know, I know). There were slots for meals and exercise, homework and reading, and some days I would even schedule coffee or movie with a friend. I was busy, and I liked it that way.

But when you are that obsessed with your schedule, you leave very little room for compassion or meaningful conversation. Whenever a lunch was running long, I fought an internal battle. I'd stop listening and start ticking off all the things on my schedule that needed to be rearranged now that my friend decided she needed a heart-to-heart. I was so unwilling to give up my time for other people.

I thought there was something wrong with me. I have always valued and loved my friends, but my schedule was running the show. I turned into this uncompassionate person who chose what she thought was best over what she really needed—a friend. I gave up life-giving moments for time alone in my room because I really needed to finish a paper that was due, not the next day, but in a week. My priorities were all out of whack.

I was still figuring out how to make time for friends, but I was also learning to prioritize quality of friends over quantity of friends. If I could invest my time in a few great relationships and worry less about all the potential friends I was missing out on, then my ability to make friendship meaningful for my schedule was within reach. Those few girl friends became my priority—and I still had plenty of time to work my on-campus job, lead small projects, and do my homework. Choosing to make them a priority freed me up to do the things I always had done before, but with less angst and pressure to try to do them all at once. There was time for friends *and* for work—and sometimes there were opportunities to do both together.

Nowadays, in this season of mothering small children, things are even more complicated. When I only have a few hours a day to pursue writing, sleeping, or keeping a home, making time for friends is challenging. So, what does shifting priorities look like at this life stage?

When Tim and I were first married, we were inseparable for about six months. We just loved spending time together (we still do!). But we also were really missing our friends. And when we became parents, the need to connect with friends became greater. We could no longer just go out at any hour and meet up with friends.

Tim and I sat down and talked about how much we value friendship. How could we prioritize each other and our family while also prioritizing our friends?

So we made a plan: We would sacrifice a night each week to let one of us do something with friends. We decided to switch off every other Thursday night. One of us stayed with Hunter, and the other person could make plans with friends.

This is a set thing in our schedule even today, a no-questions-asked time for us to connect with our people. We found the time. We made the time. We got creative about how to pursue the time. Then we kept it sacred.

THE PAIN HIDDEN IN BUSYNESS

The choice to isolate under the guise of "I'm busy" can also be a sign of a deeper issue. We all go through real seasons of hardship, pain, and heartbreak, times so overwhelming that we don't know how to reach out or ask for help from our friends. When we feel the temptation to isolate, we may use "I'm busy" as a facade for *I don't know how to deal with my pain, so I'm just going to avoid you.* But overwhelm and isolation are not a sign that we need to be left alone; they are a sign we need more support.

If you have identified that a friend of yours is masking her pain with the excuse of "being busy," she needs you. Invite her back into healthy community as much as you can. This is what Jesus does over and over. When we feel like we have messed up, made bad choices, and are not worthy of Jesus' grace and love, we often run away—but He always wants us back. Your friend might need a generous invitation to pull her out of her funk and remind her that she is loved, no matter what hard things are going on in her life. It can be easy to feel unaccepted when walking through divorce, sickness, job loss, mental-health struggles, et cetera. So, meet her in the middle. She may not want to attend your girls' night, but she may want a night in with just you, where she can be in her sweatpants. Promise to be there for her, and then follow through by showing up and being present.

The family of God is the support we often need to get through these difficult times. I love the image of Moses raising his hands to heaven when the Israelites were being attacked by the Amalekites (recounted in Exodus 17). When Moses' hands were raised, the Israelites were winning the battle. But even if you did CrossFit for a decade, you couldn't keep your hands above your head for an entire day. When Moses grew tired, his companions Aaron and Hur brought a rock for him to sit on, settled themselves on each side, and helped hold Moses' arms up for success over Israel's enemy.[4] C'mon! How can you not love this picture of friendship? When a sister is tired of the fight, we must stand next to her and help her press on. This means calling out that decision to isolate, fighting that pain of shame, and embracing her back into the family of God.

If you are the hurting friend, don't reject the invitation.

A real conversation could be the thing you need to make your bad day brighter. Your friend loves you and cares for you. Let her in to see you in the best of times and the worst of times.

God calls His people to meet regularly so we can "spur one another on toward love and good deeds."[5] I think He calls us to this because He knows we need accountability and people speaking truth over us on a regular basis to fight the fight and keep the faith.[6] God leaves the specific *how* up to us, but the *why* is simple: to be the kind of friend who embodies God's mercy, compassion, and love.

MAKING FRIENDSHIP COUNT

We must protect our time with our people—fight for togetherness—because there will be a million different things pulling and pushing for our attention. We protect the time for what matters most to us. Writing this book meant I had to say no to other things for a season because this was the priority, and it was important for me to steward this opportunity well. The same goes for our friendships. If we want friendships that count, we must model God's pursuit of relationships with people. Not only did God sacrifice His Son to have an intimate, personal relationship with us, but He gave us His Spirit, the person of God always with us. At times, we must surrender our pride, our time, our gifts, or our comfort to create intimacy in our friendships. So, when people tell me they are "too busy" to invest in their friendships, I remind them that meaningful friendship costs them something. I challenge them to be more creative. If friendship really matters to you, you will make it work.

It has taken years of practice in the art of intentionality, but now I find myself picking up my phone to call a friend when I have ten minutes in the car. I invite people to help make dinner, and I ring my neighbor's doorbell to catch up on a weekday afternoon. I write letters while my husband and I watch a favorite television show in the evenings. Amid the busyness of life, I can use pockets of time to love my friends. For you, it may look like a quick run to Target to grab Advil and flu medicine for a friend; spending a few extra minutes on a dinner for your family and a new mom; or committing to pray persistently for someone, even if it is inconvenient to your work schedule.

We won't be able to stop and serve every person or every need. But we can take one step of faith to re-evaluate where our energy and efforts to love others are being used for God's purposes. You get what you put into your friendships. Fight for togetherness.

Sole Mates

One summer in high school, a friend of ours decided he wanted to become a better runner. Well, you don't let your friends do hard things alone. So a group of us started a running club named Sole Mates to become better friends with running, better friends with each other, and better friends with Jesus. We met two evenings a week to support our friend on his new journey to run a mile in ten minutes in the Kansas heat.

Each Sole Mates date began with stretching and sharing prayer requests before we set out on the run. The mile would take some of us eight minutes, others of us twelve, but it was important that no matter what your pace was, we were all in it together. Then we'd collapse in the driveway and chat about our running playlists. One guy friend liked to run to the *Phantom of the Opera* soundtrack; who were we to judge?

Some of us were experienced runners, and some were

beginners. The goal wasn't to be the best but to have fun and support one another. We saw our friends at their worst and sweatiest, which is something that creates a different bond from just "hanging out." We shared in each other's accomplishments, had lots of fun with themed runs (like "bring your dog night"), and usually followed up with snacks. When we left for college, we tried to start Sole Mates at our individual campuses, hoping to continue health goals and friend time.

Finding a memory-making activity that draws us closer together is an excellent way to invest in our friends. If you want to connect with your friends through movement, start your own Sole Mates—matching bedazzled water bottles encouraged.

5

WHEN THE FRIENDSHIP DOESN'T MEASURE UP

Navigating Friendship Expectations

The air had turned crisp and the leaves had just started showing some yellow on the day my mom interrupted my usually scheduled program of Saturday-morning cartoons for a road trip to an antique store in a nearby town. The store was called Three French Hens. It was a charming country house with whitewashed wood panels, pumpkins lining the steps up to the porch, and lace curtains hanging in every window. The two older women who owned the place dressed like pioneers and looked like quintessential country grandmothers.

Three French Hens was a fall wonderland. As I stepped

inside, the smell of apple cider and autumn hit my nose. There were candles, ceramic chickens, burlap tablecloths, and lots of premade fall cooking kits—chili, cinnamon rolls, pumpkin bread.

My mom and I had always cherished fall, but this . . . this was our Disneyland.

Three French Hens became our special yearly tradition. Whenever I could wrap myself up in an oversized sweatshirt, I knew our favorite season had arrived! On the way, we'd listen to the Hot 100 on the radio and grab Sonic slushies. As we'd pull up, I could already taste the apple cider on my tongue. Every year we picked out at least one fall item to take home to remember our fun afternoon together.

By the time I was in middle school, I was the one asking my mom when we could visit. So, when sweater weather returned, I asked if we could visit. My mom agreed to go, so we quickly gathered our things and got in the car.

Expectations were high—I mean, how could they not be? We were going to find the perfect pumpkin to decorate the front porch, and I was going to purchase a fall-spice candle for the kitchen (start 'em young, and your kids become people who spend all their budget on candles).

But then we arrived . . . and the store *felt* different.

It seemed smaller.

The items in the shop weren't as special or unique as I remembered.

They didn't put the apple cider out that year.

Items were overpriced, and my mom and I didn't find anything in the store that looked worth purchasing, anyway.

Had the store changed ownership? Was I just remembering things differently?

Maybe my cherished memory clouded the reality of the experience. Were my expectations for our trip too high?

Looking back, I realize that nothing had really changed that year. But my build-up to the trip meant that the real thing couldn't measure up. I was disappointed and melancholy when we hopped back into the car. My mom pulled away from our favorite fall store, and I just knew somehow deep down that we wouldn't be back. Even though we didn't exchange how we felt in the moment, I could tell the store had lost a bit of its charm for my mom too. Our unmet expectations killed the experience itself.

Expectations can do that in friendship too.

FRIENDSHIP EXPECTATIONS

Have you thought about what expectations you bring to friendships? Or where those expectations come from?

Expectations form in shapes and ways we might not even be aware of:

- Entertainment sells us happy-go-lucky friendships.

- Social media shows us best friends have expensive brunches together every Saturday (and of course have matching shirts to up the BFF factor).

- Our older sister or mom tells us we'll find our "forever" friends once we get to college or start having kids . . . always a season ahead of where we are, making us wonder when it'll be our turn.

Or perhaps your unmet expectations are shaped by your past experiences:

- You loved your coworkers at your old job, but the people at your new job have been different and difficult to befriend.

- The moms at your daughter's new school aren't like the moms at your daughter's old school.

Our past friendship experiences shape our expectations for what community will be like today, and when they don't align how we imagined, an unhealthy discontent seeps in. Even if our expectations come from the best intentions, they often harm our ability to experience the life-giving community that may already be right in front of us.

German theologian Dietrich Bonhoeffer said it best:

He who loves his dream of a community more than the Christian community itself becomes a destroyer of the latter, even though his personal intentions may be ever so honest and earnest and sacrificial.[1]

When friends don't measure up to our unrealistic expectations, we often check out. It's as if the first impression is the only metric for discerning a true friend—and trust me, nobody wants to be judged as friendship material based off a first impression. This type of friendship approach is different from the healthy standards we set for friendship in chapter 2—this is an unrealistic expectation, often formed from what culture tells us friendship looks like . . . and resulting in us destroying a beautiful thing before it even happens. We may find ourselves spending more time looking for the perfect set of friends than *actually being a friend*. We shouldn't give up on community when we are disappointed by the first impressions because they can often be misleading. So, the first Bible-study group might be a little awkward or the new coworker was anxious and quiet; these unmet expectations are not grounds for dismissing a potential friend. Instead of allowing surface-level things to get in the way of great friendship, we need to acknowledge, process, and dig into our unmet expectations.

But unmet expectations don't stop at new friendships. I've also gone through my fair share of unmet expectations with some of my closest friends. Once I expected a friend to show up for one of my first speaking engagements . . . and she didn't. She wasn't trying to be rude. I hadn't communicated with her how important it was for her to be there. I placed expectations for our friendship on her without her knowledge, and when she didn't meet them, I was hurt. If I had only communicated what I thought support in a friendship looks like, then maybe the drama could have been avoided.

Has something like this ever happened to you? Maybe you are going through something hard, and your friend didn't check in on you. You expected her to be there, but maybe she thought you wanted space. There is a disconnect that leads to disappointment—a reminder that we are far from picture-perfect community.

Friendship can't feel good all the time. When you get disappointed because a friendship takes more work than you originally thought or a group of friends isn't like the actual *Friends* on television, this is probably a sign that your unhealthy expectations no longer align with godly expectations for friendship. When we go back to the basics—love God, love others, repeat—we'll find ourselves letting go of culture's expectations and embracing life together. We may get tastes of some sweet, transcendent moments with our friends, like an epic girls' trip or a conversation that left you both feeling so known and loved. But the truth is we live most of our daily lives in the mundane: texting about your dry-shampoo experiment, chatting over your lunch break, or sitting together in church on Sunday. Let's choose to be grateful for both: the mountain-top moments and the mundane reality.

God gives the gift of a friend not because that person meets all our needs, expectations, and wants but because He loves us enough to give us companions in the work of His Kingdom—what some Christians like to call "life-on-life ministry." We get to live with and love others in the body of Jesus—the arm, the eye, and the leg—despite our differences and imperfections.[2] God chooses to knit His people together, not with a shared love for iced chai lattes and indie films but with a shared love for Jesus.

When we embrace the people He has so graciously provided, we find ourselves genuinely enjoying those around us. Practicing contentment in place of complaining will create the connection we long for, even with the most unlikely friend. You'll never find a "perfect" set of friends, but you may find something even better—faithful friendship.

COMMIT TO IMPERFECT COMMUNITY

In a world where the majority response to friendship is "maybe," we get to be people who choose to say "yes"—and mean it. You know those buttons on every event invite that say "maybe"? Like *Maybe I will come to your birthday party* or *Maybe I will join you for that concert*—but the ambiguous response lingers, and we wonder: *Are you in, or are you out?*

Why are we so afraid to just say yes?

I don't want to say yes because it means I might have to participate in a social activity that is uncomfortable for me. I might be too tired to carry on a seemingly awkward conversation. I might be too shy to meet new people. Some days I want to stay home and never even attempt this thing called friendship. We can be wishy-washy about our friendships—something we care deeply about, but also something we think we don't need to tend to when we don't feel like it. In other words, being a faithful friend involves confronting my selfish tendencies, and to be honest, I don't love it.

But God invites us into friendship not solely to meet our needs and keep us in our comfort zones. God's definition for fellowship is that we can connect with anyone who proclaims to "walk in the light."[3] This means anyone is a potential friend—yes, even the women who give off a weird first impression. God is not above using imperfect people to create beautiful friendships. So even when we find ourselves having tough conversations about our unmet expectations with one another, God is there. He's in it when we struggle together for a solution to mismatched understandings of friendship. He's part of our apologies when we misunderstand each other and when we practice being more considerate next time.

He's the architect of the flourishing that happens when we align our expectations, get on the same page, and better live out our "partnership in the gospel."[4]

In God's paradigm, He doesn't tell us we will all be exactly alike; He says we will all be like-minded in Christ.[5] He does not say our friends will meet all our standards; He says we will experience mutual love when we honor others above our ourselves.[6]

"What may appear weak and trifling to us may be great and glorious to God," Dietrich Bonhoeffer challenges us to consider.[7] Unlikely friendship may initially feel like an impossibility, but any of us who have stuck with it know that God never gets the assignment wrong. When He puts someone in our path who we feel even an inkling to show kindness toward, they may be the exact person who needs a friend like us. Bonhoeffer concludes that friendship "is not an ideal which we must realize; it is rather a reality created by God in Christ in which we may participate."[8]

We move toward genuine friendship by reaching for God's vision for friendship instead of the world's shallow understanding of it. When we grasp God's commission for friendship, we are freed from our selfish tendencies and can participate in the community God has called us to—a group of people we can invest in and grow alongside.

Despite our biases and frustrations . . .

- *She's interested in the weirdest things—we have nothing in common . . .*
- *Her kids make conversations difficult . . .*
- *She always brings along that one friend I cannot stand . . .*

God sees potential for great, true friends.

Despite the mundane aspects of tending to a friendship . . .

- *All we do is sit on the couch and catch up . . .*
- *We never do anything fun or flashy like I see on social media . . .*
- *We only talk about our kids, not the book I just read or the last movie I watched . . .*

God uses those moments and builds on them.

Even when you question if your friendships are growing deeper . . .

- *Do our weekly phone calls make a difference?*
- *Does she recognize the sacrifices I make to spend time with her?*
- *Is praying for her going to change our relationship?*

God views your faithful habits as obedient steps in the right direction.

Friendship Tip: If you are struggling to have mercy or compassion for that one person in your group who is hard to love, take the position of being curious instead of critical. Getting to know someone helps us stop identifying them as an "other" and start appreciating who they are and where they are in their journey. Once we discover the best in someone, we can sincerely love them, even when they are different from ourselves.

PRAY TO BE KNIT TOGETHER

The first evening Tim and I opened our doors to our small group, I had prepped myself to set my expectations appropriately. (See, I was learning from my mistakes!) Our church encourages us to weekly walk through life with other believers based on where we live, versus whom we like best, so I really had no idea whom God was going to bring to our front steps.

Tim and I were (and still are) passionate about small-group community, and on day one we had committed to serving the community for a period of two years. Whoever showed up at our home would be part of our lives for quite some time. We knew we couldn't walk into the situation without some spiritual tools.

So, we prayed often, asking God to knit our community of strangers into a family. Whether someone came from a different denominational background, economic situation, or life stage, we wanted God to craft within our community mutual respect and affection. Not everyone was going to see this small group as a perfect fit, but we could rely on God to do what He does best and unite the church, right in our living room.

Six months into meeting, we had grown from twelve to twenty-four men and women. It was a lot to navigate, but the single most beautiful thing God did was create a real sense of care and admiration for one another. People genuinely called each other friends. Our group went from meeting on Wednesday nights to hanging out on Fridays, Sundays . . . really, you could find someone willing to go on a walk or share a meal *any* day of the week.

God took a group of strangers and created a culture of togetherness. Five years later, we have retired as official leaders—and three small groups have launched from our original group because of people passionate about sharing this quality connection with others in our city. Our small group was not perfect—far from it. But at our last evening together, many shared how they were frightened to open up to a bunch of unfamiliar people, but when they decided to come every week and engage, they gained a family they could count on.

And we have felt the same. Some of our closest friends have come out of this group. City living is idyllic but also lonely. We would not have planted our roots in Denver, away from our families, if it weren't for this spiritual family that has developed here.

What made all the difference for us and our people? God's affection. If we want to *see* the potential friends God has put right in front of us, we need to ask God for an affection for the people around us. Affection, in the words of C. S. Lewis, "gives itself no airs . . . can love the unattractive . . . 'does not expect too much' . . . revives easily after quarrels . . . opens our eyes to goodness we could not have seen, or should not have appreciated without it."[9]

As people who are made in the image of God, [10] we each exhibit who God is in different ways. Can we look for the characteristics of God in our friends? Can we respect and give our new friends the benefit of the doubt even when they mess up, disappoint us, forget to call us back, or just have an "off" day?

Coming to our friendships without crazy expectations is one step, but taking it further—choosing to actively look for, recognize, and encourage the best parts in our friends—is a game changer.

I'm not saying you should blindly overlook real sin and faults in their lives. But seeing people the way God sees them softens our hearts to enjoy the community we are in.

This passage from Ephesians often reminds me what God does for us in friendship:

From whom the whole body, joined and held
together by every joint with which it is equipped,

when each part is working properly, makes the body grow so that it builds itself up in love.[11]

Those of us who decide to say yes to faithful friendship can experience the joy of God knitting unlikely people together—not to meet our expectations but to promote growth in God's love. When we are prayerful about our friendships, God can use ordinary beginnings to make friendship extraordinary.

FRIENDSHIP PEP TALK:
Don't Give Up

And let us not grow weary of doing good,
for in due season we will reap,
if we do not give up.

GALATIANS 6:9

6

FRIENDS FOR A SEASON

When Change Enters the Equation

When change happens, it costs us something. We lose a piece of what is familiar, so we avoid the pain of change as much as possible. When we experience change in our friendships, it's normal to cling to "the way things have always been" because we are afraid to lose what we have. Is it possible change could grow your friendships for the better? And is there a way to navigate the changes that end a friendship for good?

What kind of changes threaten the status quo of our friendships? The shift in our seasons of life can be anything:

- A friend moved away, and your communication has become scarce.
- Someone got married, and it feels like they don't have time for you anymore.
- Your roommate started a new friendship, and she seems to want to spend more time with the new girl instead of you.
- Your friend just became a mom, and you really feel left out of her life.

These harmless transitions can make us question: *Am I no longer a priority for them? What does this mean for our friendship? Am I losing them?*

Our impulse is to treat change as a death. We assume that a friendship either needs to be "on" or "off." When a new season keeps her busy, we often don't pivot or consider new rhythms for spending time together—we just stop.

This was the fear I held when becoming a mom—that my friends would just stop being my friends. When I sat down with a close friend to tell her I was pregnant, I was terrified. Because it was already an unexpected adjustment for me, I only imagined how this would affect her and our friendship. She was caught off guard, genuinely sad because our cherished free time together was going to change. What was my new season going to mean for the longevity of our relationship? Would we let this be the thing that stalled our friendship?

FINDING NEW RHYTHMS

Changing seasons often set off a chain reaction in our friendships, and we may find ourselves doing one of two things:

1. Trusting God and adjusting; or
2. Lashing out, blaming, or threatening the friendship because we feel hurt.

Our response usually reveals the heart reaction behind the friendship and the true state of its health.

My friend who was nervous about a baby getting between us had legitimate feelings. I was just as nervous about this new schedule being a friend repellant. When the baby came, it was a new season for me to navigate meeting the needs of a baby, a husband, *and* my other relationships.

There were times when I thought she was pulling back, investing in other friends more than in me (after all, who wants to go to happy hour with a crying newborn?). But just as the height of insecurities would rise, something would shift—her work schedule was more flexible, we had a girls' night, or she called me about something she wanted to process—and we'd find ourselves spending time together again. Perhaps things were not the same as before, but our friendship was still fruitful and life-giving.

The more I communicated that I wanted to spend time with her, the more she felt like I was opening the doors to let her back in to the chaos of everyday life. We reached a healthier understanding of what we expected from the relationship—we wanted to remain close, so we created rituals for our relationship that worked for us. Every Thursday night, she'd come over and we'd watch a favorite show together and catch up. We'd still meet at a coffee shop or go on a walk on other occasions, but for the eight weeks of our television program, we set apart time to connect amid our busy lives.

You don't have to be a new mom to feel this way about your friends. Sometimes women just pull away as things change in their faith, dating life, or priorities. As seasons change, we don't need to abandon a friendship—we learn to make new rhythms. Let's put it this way: The things you used to do to connect with your friends in high school probably didn't work for creating community in college, right? And the habits you had for friend building in college may not work as you embark on a career or move to a new city. Change, big or little, will require some creativity and understanding in our friendships.

Sacrifice Comforts

To cultivate your friendships in new seasons, you may need to sacrifice a comfort. If you started a new job that keeps you working later than you expected, you may need to get up early some mornings to connect with friends. If you are a mom of multiple kids, you may need to ask your spouse or hire a sitter to help you set aside time with friends. Or if you're in a season where you're feeling extra tired, sometimes all you need is to turn off Netflix and grab your car keys to go meet a friend.

A recent study at the University of Texas found that frequent ten-minute phone calls decreased people's loneliness by *20 percent.*[1] This is huge! Our mental health is dependent on offering small windows to connect with friends throughout the week. So don't be alarmed when trying something new feels intimidating; big, over-the-top gestures aren't always necessary to maintain your friendships. Instead, regularly tending to your friends helps you find healthier rhythms for all of you.

Know Your Limits

We cannot *be* everything and *do* everything for our friends. What we can do is evaluate our time, resources, and commitments. Things change: work projects change, family needs change, finances change—it is okay to take these things into consideration when finding new rhythms to build your friendships. (And remember: Boundaries change from season to season. You may need to evaluate your friendship rhythms several times over the course of your life.)

Be realistic with your limits. Don't plan to do ten coffee dates a week if you know that isn't feasible for your schedule and budget. Don't promise to sit in the stands and cheer on your friend's son at every soccer game if you know you can't (or don't want to) do that. Recognize what season you are in and let your friends know what you can and cannot do.

My limits change constantly as the needs of my small children change. I can't always come and pick a friend up at the airport because it is an-hour-and-a-half journey during dinnertime, but on a Sunday afternoon during nap time, sure. I communicate clearly with my friends about what I can and cannot do so they know that while I'm not always available, I still care about the relationship.

Communicate Openly

Don't expect your friends to always know how your life season has affected your friendship. I had been a mom for years when a good friend asked, "Do you ever feel like we don't invite you to do friend stuff with us because you are a mom?"

"Of course," I said. "It would be hard not to feel that way when you all know I can't go to a weeknight concert or do another girls' day because I promised my husband to work on house stuff that day. I understand why you don't invite me because usually I can't go, but . . . I still wish you'd extend the invite. If you give me enough advance notice, I can often make things work."

She nodded. "I am really sorry I have left you out. I just assume you aren't available, so I don't think to ask you. I just had the thought pop into my mind today. I am sorry. I am going to be better about inviting you to things."

Our honest conversation allowed me to express that I wanted my friends to include me in activities. And I was freed to communicate my limits without her assuming I was too busy to connect in my current life phase.

Open and honest communication amid changing seasons is vital. We need to have faith that our friends will carry our reality well—and that requires sharing our needs. And they need to trust that we'll hear their concerns as they adapt to new seasons or navigate ours alongside us.

Talk about your limits in your new season. Be clear—the sooner the better. Silence is a friendship killer! Don't allow the tension of changing seasons push you apart when open conversation could quickly help you reach mutual ground.

NOSTALGIC VERSUS ADAPTIVE FRIENDSHIP

Friendships won't stay the same forever because time and experience change *us*. We learn a lot about ourselves when we're transitioning into new jobs, cities, relationships, or communities.

The summer after I moved to Denver, I went to my hometown to visit friends, and things felt different. We tried to re-create our old, choreographed dances, visit the same spots in town, and pretend we were still sixteen . . . but we were twenty-two. Nothing was quite the same. The moments felt forced, and I began to question where our friendships would go from there. Would they adapt and mature as we grew as young adults, or would they become a fond memory?

One of the worst things we can do is put our friends in a box of "who they once were" and expect the friendship to function like it had before. Secretly, we want our friends to be predictable. But *nostalgic friendship only allows our friendship to function in the past, without freedom to mature or grow.*

I've found myself stuck in nostalgic friendships that are not life-giving because we're both too nervous to try something new, to say something we're afraid the other person won't understand, or to admit that we have outgrown the friendship.

But healthy relationships can emerge if we acknowledge that our personalities, interests, and habits adjust over time. This is *adaptive friendship: the ability to embrace the change in our friends and make it our mission to love them in all their various roles and life seasons.* When we can adapt, ask good questions, and keep learning things about our friends, then we create a setting for *life-long* friendships.

My hometown friends and I decided to *adapt*—and they have remained some of my closest connections, even though we only see one another a few times a year. After some practice, we began to understand the changes and appreciate the new things about each other.

Consider a longtime friendship in your life. Is it a nostalgic friendship that is meant to remain a fond memory, or an adaptive friendship that's willing to recognize that people change? It can be hard to let go of nostalgic friendships because they are exactly that: nostalgic! They remind you of all the good times. But these types of friendships have morphed into ambivalent relationships that are harmful to preserve. You don't really know if this friend is reliable or not. Author and researcher Lydia Denworth noted that when we feel supported and have someone we know we can count on, our mental and physical health improves. But trying to maintain an ambivalent friendship is worse than just letting ourselves part ways.[2] So as you change and grow, releasing nostalgic friends may be what you need to find capacity for the new ones you are creating.

Don't feel shame for the friendship growing apart. Instead, recognize the significance of the role they played in your life at a time you needed them most. Nostalgic friends helped build a piece of who you are; they are an important part of your history. Friends who are a safe place for you to grow are the keepers!

If you sense a friend has made new priorities in her life season and isn't willing to give back to the friendship the way that you want, release that too. *Don't chase after people God has not assigned to you.* Perhaps you are *their* just-for-a-season friend. Be confident that God will continue to open doors for you to create new connections and find friends that fit your new rhythms for friendship.

Podcast and Pizza Party

Keeping activities affordable, simple, and fun is the key to sustaining fresh ways to connect with your friends. Tim and I stumbled on a great idea one day when we were brainstorming our next joint friend gathering.

I ran through my usual list of things that make getting together become more work than I want to sign myself up for:

- We have two kids to entertain.
- I hate cooking.
- I want people to come over to our home without all the fuss.
- I don't want to overspend for a simple afternoon with friends.

That's when it hit me: *What if we created a book club—but with podcasts?* People are often too busy to sit and read a two-hundred-page book (thanks for sitting down and reading mine, by the way), but anyone can listen to a thirty-minute podcast. Tim and I love discussing the topics or ideas podcasts offer, so why not try it with our friends? And remember how I hate cooking? We'll just order pizza!

Thus, our "Pizza and Podcast" party was born. No matter your life season, friendship blossoms when you connect with good conversation and good food.

Hosting Your Pizza and Podcast Party

- Choose a podcast that will spark some healthy conversation. For example, Tim and I chose Malcolm Gladwell's podcast *Revisionist History* because Gladwell likes to push the boundaries on many popular topics—always leaving room for a good debate.

- Send a text invite and make sure to include the link to the podcast. We invited eight people because we wanted to keep the group small. For an intimate get-together like this, you want everyone's voice to be heard, so inviting six to eight guests is perfect.

- Provide the pizza (and a salad) for everyone.

- Put a start and end time on the event to respect the importance of the conversation and have a clear cutoff.

Why This Friend Date Is a Win

- You can gather a diverse group of friends who may have not met before and discuss a topic with your varied backgrounds. No one needs prior expertise to contribute to the conversation.

- A podcast doesn't cost money to listen to. It's accessible and doesn't require much prep from guests.

- If you have a group of brainy friends, they will love this.

- This is doable with kids. Ours loved the pizza and played while we continued the conversation at the table. Older kids may enjoy joining the discussion.

- If it is well received, you can rotate hosts and do it again.

7

BETTER TO GIVE
THAN TO RECEIVE

Living in God's Friendship Economy

Do you ever feel like you contribute more to your relationship than your friend does?

Friendship expert Shasta Nelson asked this question in a survey, and the response was overwhelming: "Only 26 percent [of survey participants] feel the giving is shared equally, and a whopping 60 percent of us believe we do most of the giving in our relationships. Even the 26 percent who view *their* relationships as mutual tend to believe other women are more likely to be takers than givers."[1]

So, over half of women believe they are contributing *more*

in their friendships than their friends? This disproportionate conclusion leads me to believe it is very likely some of us are giving a lot to one friendship while also taking advantage of another.

We've all heard the cliché "it is better to give than to receive"—and yes, it's exhilarating to see a smile on someone's face and to know you did something to make your community better. But when it comes to the economy of friendship, giving more than you receive can feel terrible. When you feel like you're in a one-sided friendship, it's easy to believe your friend doesn't care enough about you to contribute equal effort.

Maybe you make the effort to initiate time together, but she never sends the first text. Or perhaps you helped her move into her new home, but when it was your turn to move, she was too preoccupied with a work thing to help.

This feeling of painful imbalance causes unforeseen damage to a friendship.

When our efforts and intentionality aren't returned, we may want to give up on friendship entirely.

- *If our friendship isn't important to her, then it is no longer important to me.*
- *I just can't give more than I am already giving. I am quitting this friendship.*

- *It's her turn to put some energy into our friendship and show me that I matter to her!*

I get it. It can be exhausting to extend ourselves over and over. My heart hardens when I feel like a friend doesn't care as much as I care or initiate like I initiate. But ultimately, we have the choice of whether we're going to carry the self-imposed burden of *I do the most in this relationship.*

When we live with our bitter frustration long enough, we start to distance ourselves from our friend—the opposite of striving for togetherness. We wonder if we can trust her enough to continue investing in a friendship that feels unequal. The solution seems clear to us: Our friends need to recognize our value and put in more effort.

But will that really solve the issue at hand? What if the issue is less about tracking who gives more to the friendship . . . and more about our *approach* to friendships?

When we come into friendships expecting to get back exactly what we put in, we create an unsustainable relational dynamic. No friendship will ever completely balance the scales, so we need to find a different way to measure trust in our friendship, one outside of who is giving the most.

GOD'S FRIENDSHIP ECONOMY

When we look at our first friendship, we see disparity in who gives more to the relationship. God is merciful, compassionate, sufficient, and generous . . . always![2] He is never not on the side of His people. He is working out all things for our good.[3] He delivers us from our sin over and over as we stumble along, and He never severs relationship when we fall short. We forget God; we reject Him; we demand He give us what we want.

And yet God is never stingy with His love and care. The apostle Paul reminds us: "Though he [Jesus] was rich, yet for your sake he became poor, so that you by his poverty might become rich."[4]

We receive this blessing in our first friendship . . . and then what do we do with it? Do we love our friends generously? Or do we, with bitter and unchanging hearts, expect our friends to match everything we're putting into the friendship? God calls us to charitable love, but we're tempted to be miserly toward our friends when we believe they're taking our love for granted.

But God's economy shows us that sacrificing for others is a priceless act of love. He calls us to consider others above ourselves not because it's the right thing to do but because we are to emulate Jesus who "did not count equality with God a thing to be grasped, but emptied himself, by taking the form of a servant."⁵ Thankfully, God's economy of friendship does not depend on our will but on His power to "equip [us] with everything good that [we] may do his will."⁶

With God's strength, our friendships can be marked by these characteristics:

- *We give to our friends without holding "interest" over them.*⁷ When a friend is in a bad place spiritually, physically, or emotionally, we are to support them without keeping a record of what they will owe us in the future. How do we accomplish this? God will supply us with a heart that is ready to give: "God is able to make all grace abound to you, so that having all sufficiency in all things at all times, you may abound in every good work."⁸

- *We give to our friends because we love them.* "For God so loved the world, that he gave his only Son."⁹ This verse, which beautifully explains the gospel, also communicates something about God's generosity. Love pours out from a full cup. Fully satisfied in God's love for us, our hearts are moved to give to others without keeping score.

• *We give to our friends out of God's abundance.* It can feel scary to give what we don't have, but God works in our giftings and seasons so we may have an abundance of what our friend lacks. As 2 Corinthians 8 says, giving should not be a burden, but "your abundance at the present time should supply their need, so that their abundance may supply your need, that there may be fairness."[10]

You will find yourself in seasons where you have more to give—more time, more hope, more prayer, more money. And other times, you will find yourself in need of your friend's generous love.

We don't have to judge the value of our friendships based on who can give the most. Instead, when we focus on giving our life away, we find that life is given back.[11] God's economy proves rich in relationship.

FROM SCARCITY TO ABUNDANCE

Healthy friendships grow when we shift our mindset from scarcity to abundance. The more we pour into a friend, the more we find ourselves also benefitting.

Whenever I initiate with a friend (give), I *receive* quality time, laughter, fun, memories, and meaningful conversation.

My one action yields the life-giving fruit I desire from my friendships.

We all have that one friend who always needs an extra nudge to get together. I text mine to grab coffee once a month. She isn't a star initiator, but she has told me that my efforts mean so much to her. Our friendship is important to her, too, despite her need to prioritize making plans ahead of time.

I am the friend who needs a plan. I need to coordinate with my husband so he can handle breakfast and getting the kids dressed for school. Texting first to align with her schedule is a necessity for me. For my friend, advance notion isn't as necessary; a coffee date with me may be a last-minute thought when she finds an opening in her work schedule.

Am I annoyed? Hurt by her lack of intentionality? Sure, sometimes I am.

But with an abundance mindset, I won't punish her for not giving more when I know I have the downtime in my day to reach out.

An abundance mindset also helps us pay attention to how friends give love. I may send the first text because that's what I want her to be doing. She may pay for my coffee because that's what she wants me to be doing for her. We often give to our friends in ways that make us feel most loved, so it is important to talk about how a friend feels loved and what giving looks like to her. You may both be giving your own version of love, but it isn't translating. Aim to understand what makes your friend feel valued as you learn more about one another.[12]

Finally, not everyone has a history with healthy give-and-take friendships. If you continue to wrestle with a one-sided giving in your friendship, it is likely your friend has never had a strong friendship experience before. You may be providing her with her first example of a godly friendship, so offer grace. Ask her about her friendship experiences before. How did her previous friends make time for each other, and how did they communicate about this? You get the opportunity to show her an example of an intentional relationship.

ONE-SIDED FRIENDSHIP

I looked down at my phone. It had been a full week since I sent the text. I reread it just to make sure I didn't say anything awkward or weird.

> Hey Kendal![13] I really enjoyed getting to know you over coffee. I would love to do it again sometime. Maybe we can go on a walk around the park. Let me know when you are free next.

It didn't seem too pushy, right? Why hadn't she texted me back? Maybe I put the number in my phone incorrectly. Maybe she wasn't interested in being friends.

I thought we'd had a really great conversation. We connected over our techy husbands, our love for hiking, and how we both struggled to make friends in a new place. I thought for sure the situation was ripe for a potential new friend. But when my follow-up text didn't get a response either, I got the message: She must not have felt the same way.

Trying to be a good friend when someone doesn't reciprocate can be painful. And as important as it is to give grace in the friendship economy, you also shouldn't find yourself completely depleted by a friend when you know she is not returning any of your efforts—or is even giving you the cold shoulder.

In my situation, disappointed didn't really sum up how I felt. Embarrassed, insecure, and unlovable is more like it. And the fading interest doesn't always happen in the beginning stages of a friendship. Sometimes we go up and down with a friend for months or years before we finally admit to ourselves that the friendship is more one-sided.

Or, worse . . . sometimes I have been the friend who decided to stop investing in the friendship and didn't communicate about it.

It's not always personal. The person might live far away, or your schedules make it difficult to invest in your friendship on a regular basis. We find ourselves prioritizing other friendships and either ignore her invites or make up reasons to not hang out until the friend stops initiating.

In this case, the one-sided friendship needs to be addressed. Otherwise the vague reasons for not engaging in a friendship can really hurt someone. Sometimes respecting people looks like naming the hard truth.

Talk about It, Not around It

Super profound, I know. But assumptions almost always create misunderstanding. To avoid missing each other's intentions, *talk about it*. If you think a friend is purposely ignoring you or has made way too many excuses each time you try to hang out, then ask them if you can talk. Let them know how the ignored messages or cancelled plans have made you feel. Ask why they have responded to your invitations this way. Be willing to hear their reasons and pray for a bridled tongue.

If someone asks you, "Are you ignoring me?" it's time to be honest. In Matthew 5:37, Jesus says to "Let what you say be simply 'Yes' or 'No.'" Often people make rash oaths to commit to things they don't plan on seeing through to the end. Likewise, we shouldn't say we are going to be a better friend if we don't mean it. If you truly don't see yourself investing in the friendship, you need to say so.

Sometimes relationships naturally end, like the gal who never texted me back. But if you still want to clarify the unspoken tension and see if there's an opportunity to reconcile, you should request a conversation.

Moving Forward with Your Friend

A hard conversation doesn't have to mean the end of the friendship. We should always seek to reconcile the friendship, even if the ultimate result doesn't look quite like what we hoped. If we don't strive for peace, then we leave room for hurt to reside in our heart and that ongoing hurt will carry into all our future friendships.

When I use the word *reconcile*, I mean the choice to actively pursue forgiveness and overall cordialness toward each other. I'm not suggesting faking your friendship or forgetting what has happened—we should do everything we can to make the situation right.

If your friend follows Jesus, she is a sister in the family of God—and family strives for unity. But more likely, you are probably going to run into this friend again. Awkward. She might go to your church, work in your office, or is friends with your tight-knit friend group. You will want to have done everything you can to honor the other person by listening, offering forgiveness, and trying to find common ground. Trust me when I tell you: This is crucial if you want to be able to peaceably do life side-by-side.

Ask God to help you see your friend as He sees her. Pray for her good.

Forgiveness doesn't always come wrapped up in a perfect bow. Peace doesn't happen overnight. A settled heart over a broken friendship can take months or years. Give yourself time to heal.

If this conversation is the turning point for both of you to kick it into friendship gear, awesome! Forgive and begin taking those healing steps forward. You have repented, which means you have promised to *change* your friendship habits with this person.

But when the forecast shows storms ahead, then both people need to extend the humility needed to close the doors completely on the friendship.

Moving Forward without Your Friend

Not every friendship is meant to continue through every phase of your life. It's not a failure if one of you moves on without the other. If you're the one who has been pulling back and you know you don't want to reengage in the friendship, you can say something like, "I am really sorry; I haven't been a good friend and I have made excuses. I don't think I have the time to invest in this friendship right now." Clear. Honest. No wiggle room to misinterpret the future of this friendship. But also, still kind.

When a friend is honest with you about not seeing a future for the friendship, it's important to respect her decision. Easier said than done, right? But if someone isn't interested in being a committed friend, then we probably don't want them as a friend. There's no reason to stay in a friendship that unnecessarily hurts your feelings because you think maybe they will have more time for you in the future. By choosing to respect the end of one friendship, you are making space to find friends who are willing to go deep with you.

GIVING GROWS GOOD FRUIT

We want to see good fruit grow from the tending and pruning of our friendships. Yet we can't expect to reap the rewards of something we have not invested in ourselves. Halfhearted efforts will produce shallow foundations for these relationships—making us frustrated with our progress. Even though it feels countercultural, nurturing our friendships by serving others is exactly what develops deep-rooted friendships. Let's remember the first rule of God's friendship economy: "It is more blessed to give than to receive."[14]

Even when you feel like your welcome went unnoticed, trust that your faithfulness to hospitality made all the difference for someone else.

Unseen Moments

Friendships flourish in the unseen moments of hospitality:

- making space in your calendar
- inviting and planning ahead
- cleaning your home before hosting
- praying for meaningful conversation
- decorating for a warm environment
- cooking the meal
- picking up the check
- making a long drive to meet them halfway
- cleaning up after the party
- remembering the special occasion

8

STICKS AND STONES

When Words Cut Deep

In middle school, Anne of Green Gables captured my heart.[1] A quirky redhead with a vivid imagination, Anne knows how to make her own fun, and she cherishes her friendships with a fierce appreciation and loyalty.

When Anne first moves to Prince Edward Island, she asks her new friend Diana if she will be her *bosom friend*. The bosom is the heart, the place where we keep our most secret thoughts and feelings. A bosom friend is one you could trust to know all of you and feel safe that they won't turn your words and thoughts against you. To my twelve-year-old self, in the messy, gossipy middle-school years, this was the epitome of a friend. This bosom friend would agree to be loyal despite the embarrassing things I might wear and would promise to always be there, even if we'd had a disagreement the day before about who would be allowed to marry our favorite pop star someday.

But *finding* a lasting bosom friend doesn't come without its complications. All through school (and beyond), I met girls who were just plain mean. They said petty things because they were jealous or intentionally wanted me to feel "less than." As I got older, I often struggled with women who disingenuously promised we would get together but never contacted me and excluded me from their group. Even a close friend can sometimes hurt my feelings, intentionally or not, which turns my whole narrative upside down.

How could she?

I trusted her!

I thought she was my friend!

When we were kids playing at the playground, parents and schoolteachers told us that "sticks and stones will break my bones, but words will never hurt me." Adults tell this to kids to give them control over who can hurt their feelings or not. But unfortunately, the "cute" cliché only covers the surface of the real damage being done: What someone says to us has the potential to sink down deep and hurt us fiercely. Some people might be able to just throw off hurtful things, confident in who they are, but for many of us, hurtful words and actions can be hard to shake.

As much as we hope to outgrow this season, the playground cattiness of elementary school gets translated to social media, where adults judge, gossip, and say mean things to one another.

We often see women as our greatest champions, but they can also create some deep wounds. Our friends will let us down. They will forget the important things and remember the petty things. Women will intentionally or unintentionally leave us out and may tell a sarcastic joke that feels a bit too personal. One day things may seem great, and the next day, a friend posts a picture of her brunch date with everyone in your friend group but you.

I truly thought I could leave the immature drama behind when I finished school, but unfortunately mean-girl moments are a reality. (Note that I say *moments* because we have all been that mean girl in some insecure/petty/jealous moment. We aren't perfect.) They're an inevitable piece of the human experience. Our world is broken, including our relationships. This means conflict, hurt feelings, misunderstandings, and mean-spiritedness will sometimes emerge in our friendships. How are we to pursue meaningful friendship, knowing mean-filled situations will come?

DON'T OWN WHAT ISN'T YOURS

A risky piece of friendship is letting someone know us so intimately that they also know what we are most sensitive about. Their words can highlight our insecurities and awaken our inner critic, making us believe things we have always feared were true about ourselves.

Once, I cried for days over a friend's harsh words because I could not understand where her frustration had originated from and why she was taking it out on me. She had been in a friend group of mine for years. Yet, in just a few weeks, her attitude towards the group had turned negative. She said that my family had never been welcoming to her and our group was surface level at best. These words hurt so much because I knew all the effort we'd put in to making people feel accepted and comfortable in that particular friend group. I was devasted. If she felt that way, then did everyone else feel that way too? I played the words over and over in my mind, doubting every friendship in the group I had. I believed that if one person felt this way, then everyone must feel this way about me.

At night, I couldn't stop replaying all our conversations

and one-on-one hangouts. Had it all been a lie? Had she never really liked me? For weeks, I drove myself crazy trying to figure out where I went wrong.

I became insecure in all my relationships. When another friend didn't text back right away, I would panic internally. Maybe she had decided to stop being my friend too. As I watched the former friend spend time with our mutual friends, I wondered if she was gossiping about me and trying to get them to turn against me. I didn't feel safe. I didn't feel loved. I didn't feel accepted.

I am a confident woman, secure in Christ, surrounded by quality friends—but this one woman's experience, which was true for her, wrecked me.

I knew where I needed to be—in my Bible—but I could not silence my thoughts enough to concentrate on what I read. After some weeks, I finally slow-crawled to my Bible and sought to replace those hurtful words with God's Word:

- You are a child of God.
- You are a friend of Jesus.
- You are accepted by Jesus.
- You are redeemed and forgiven by the grace of Jesus.
- You are God's workmanship.
- You are light.

- You have the peace of God to guard your heart and mind.
- You have all your needs met in God.
- You belong to God.
- You are loved by God.[2]

Slowly, I began building myself back up in truth. I prayed often that God would bring sweet encouragements from my friends to remind me that they cared. And God totally did. I began to regain my God-given confidence. I knew I was loved even if not every person understood my intentions or liked the way I chose to be a friend.

When you are in the throes of friendship struggles, find a safe friend you can trust to share your pain, someone who can speak truth over you. Whether they text you a Scripture verse every day for a week or tell you to your face what God thinks about you, try to find friends who can hold you up in God's truth.

In this particular situation, I took the healing step of asking a friend outside of my community—and the state of Colorado—to hear my questions and insecurities. She was a voice I could rely on: someone who loved me enough to encourage but not automatically take my side.

Don't own what isn't yours to carry. Women sometimes

say mean things, and we may never know their motivation. What God says about you is true, and those things are really the most important things about you.

OWN WHAT IS YOURS

We all mess up. Sometimes we give in to frustration or a buried mean streak and say things we wish we hadn't. Sometimes we become so focused on ourselves and our own lives that we forget to think about our friends. I have been annoyed by a friend's comment and replied with unwarranted snark. I have initiated gossip about a friend just because I wanted to share my thoughts and personal judgments. I have hurt friends by forgetting important dates.

Once a friend came over to catch up, and as we talked and laughed, she paused and said, "Hey, I don't want to bring this up, but you forgot my birthday. And I don't really need presents or a big celebration, but you didn't even text me. I expect that from some of my other friends, but not you. And it hurt my feelings."

Ugh! I was just torn up. But I was also so proud of my friend for owning her hurt feelings and being bold enough to confront me. I needed to be bold in return: to own what I did and apologize.

"I am beyond sorry," I said. "You are so important to

me. I love celebrating birthdays, and I would never miss an opportunity to celebrate you, but I just forgot. It wasn't in my calendar, and I didn't get one of those helpful Facebook notifications. I just forgot, and I am sorry it hurt your feelings. It wasn't intentional. Could you remind me of the date? It's going in my calendar right now so I never forget again."

I brought her a gift the next time I saw her because I love giving gifts. And because I wanted to right the wrong. I cared about this friend, and I wanted her to know I valued her despite my forgetfulness.

Own what you did. As well as, own your pain and responsibility to speak up, like my friend did. When we admit our friendship flaws, we display how much we value the friendship over our own pride. Because a good friendship isn't about being right in the situation, it's about finding a way to reconcile the wrongs.

If you're the one who got hurt, know that sometimes you need to let an offense go, knowing that it was not personal or that your friend was having a bad day or simply didn't realize their behavior was hurtful. But sometimes you do need to address the issue—preferably by talking through the issue in person, removing as many barriers to misunderstanding one another as possible. A great posture to take is to stand *with* your friend, not against her. Picture yourself standing side-by-side with her and working through the hard things together (versus standing opposite from her). Your togetherness is more important than your "otherness." You *want* to be on her side, to understand her hurt, to give her the benefit of the doubt, with a "we are on the same team" mentality.

TAKING A BREAK FROM A FRIENDSHIP

When the wounds feel fresh, taking a step back to reevaluate the safety of your friendship can be healthy. You need time to rebuild trust. As author Van Moody wrote in *The People Factor*, "Regardless of the many reasons for a separation, we sometimes need to ask or allow someone who has been a valuable or even vital part of our lives to leave the relationship because a once-positive association has become negative."[3] When a friend fails to see the hurt they have caused, sometimes attempting to reconnect too soon only leaves you feeling anxious. There's a difference between befriending a bully and learning to forgive a friend for a mean comment. Don't confuse the two. It's not wise or safe to entrust your heart to someone who is uninterested in treating it well. This would be the beginning steps toward an unhealthy, toxic friendship. Even though you had the intention of staying friends through thick and thin, taking a break from regular, intimate conversation gives you the opportunity to discern which direction this friendship is heading—positively or negatively.

WHEN WOUNDS LEAD TO CONNECTION

We can choose to be a better friend because someone has been a bad one. Remembering what those negative experiences were like, we can take mean-girl moments and turn them into meaningful connection:

For all the moments you didn't belong, choose to invite that girl sitting by herself.

For all the times someone said something mean about the way you look, say five kind things to someone else.

For all the evenings you sat at home feeling left out, make plans for a girls' night.

For all the lonely days you wish you had someone to talk to, create trust and invite deep conversation with your roommate.

For all the seasons you have struggled to find healthy community, remember that God has placed women in your local community who are genuine, friendly, and kindhearted.

And if the only thing that came out of a bad friendship experience was drawing you closer to God, then that alone is still profoundly good. God's loving-kindness is waiting for you in the middle of every hurt. God doesn't let mean-girl moments go unseen or unredeemed.

In addition to fighting mean-girl culture, we should also reflect on how our words affect the quality of our friendships.

Our tongue, though it may be the smallest part of our bodies, can do serious damage to our friendships.[4] James says it best: "With it [our tongue] we bless our Lord and Father, and with it we curse people who are made in the likeness of God."[5] One minute we are friendly to our friend's face, and the next moment, we are jealous for something she posted about herself on social media. We are tempted to screenshot it and send it to another friend in hopes that she will join us in judging that other friend mercilessly behind her back. I know I've been guilty of it.

As women who love Jesus, we cannot spread rumors or condone words that put others down. It is contradictory to who we are in Jesus and calls into question if we truly know how loved we are by God—because if we did, we would do everything we can to hold up our sisters in Christ and draw women to the faith who do not yet know the kindness of God. We want our words to reflect the positive work God is doing in us, for "whoever says he is in the light and hates his brother is still in darkness. Whoever loves his brother abides in the light, and in him there is no cause for stumbling."[6] Abiding in the light of God gives us the security to shine a light on others. Our words of praise and encouragement are not ingenuine when we know God has made each of us for a specific purpose . . . and that we achieve these things better together. Instead of relying on mean-spirited acts to make you feel more important, you can create a safe space for *everyone* to feel known and accepted as they are—assured they can be their true selves without the fear of being teased. Supporting each other protects the vulnerability it takes for us to grow meaningful connection.

FRIENDSHIP PEP TALK:
You Made a Difference

You made a difference in your friendships this year.

- You made a new friend.
- You traveled long distances to stay connected.
- You brought monster cookies when she called about her bad day.
- You started a Bible study to go deeper in God's Word.

- You wore matching T-shirts to prove you were on the same team.
- You rallied for a friend who was sick and needed extra help around the house.
- You wrote a note of encouragement.
- You were intentional with your time.
- You approached the girl sitting by herself.
- You traveled miles by car and plane to make it to her special occasion.
- You knelt beside the girl who needed support.
- You prayed dozens of prayers.
- You forgave when it was difficult.
- You had a sleepover just because.
- You offered an apology despite the nerves you felt.
- You made a meal for a new mom.
- You had more caffeine than you could have fathomed, but the coffee dates were worth it.
- You hosted a game night.
- You listened well.
- You gave wise words of advice.
- You stepped into a new community even when it felt scary and hard.
- You confronted a friend about a tough situation with humility and kindness.

- You made posters and stood by the finish line.
- You celebrated their victories.
- You cried through their losses.
- You laughed more than you knew you could.
- You served together.
- You showed up for the important things *and* the unimportant things.
- You loved like Jesus.
- *You left a mark on your people this year!*

9

SHOW YOUR SWEAT STAINS

Choosing Vulnerability

"Show your people your sweat stains." My eyes quickly moved up from my phone to the man speaking on stage. I was attending a leadership conference, and the speakers had begun to blur together as the day dragged on.

But when the man spoke, the entire church auditorium grew silent.

Who wants to show their sweat stains—ever? There are entire commercials about avoiding sweat stains—and shirts designed to hide them from the public eye. So why was this man asking us to show the most embarrassing, and often uncontrollable, parts of our bodies to people?

He continued, "Show your people your weaknesses, your flaws, and you will gain their trust to move forward together."[1] Okay, now I get it! He was talking about vulnerability. The more we show our true selves, sweaty pits and all, the more we will create healthy, trusting relationships that propel us forward—that get us talking to people's hearts rather than just their heads. Trust gives us room to disagree without threat, celebrate without envy, and share disappointment without being considered a failure.

We want friendship to feel like a tight-knit team; we want mutual growth and like-mindedness. We desire to go through life together, not as carbon copies, but "having the same love, being united in full accord and of one mind."[2] We want to feel safe to express our different opinions and share our mistakes, knowing the foundation of our friendship won't crumble at the first sign of disagreement. We want the depth that comes with healthy communication patterns.

But we may not be sure how to get there. We ask ourselves:

- *How can I deepen my friendships to the point where we can share anything with each other?*
- *How can I make a new friendship feel like a best friendship in a short amount of time?*

• *How can my small group grow close enough to talk about our real struggles?*

My response is simple: Show your sweat stains.

Vulnerability is like adding lighter fluid to the flame of friendship—you're going to heat things up much faster than sitting back and waiting for the logs to catch fire. Sharing the real issues allows

• long-distant friendships to remain close,
• current friendships to explore new connection points, and
• budding friendships to cultivate trust.

Why? Because you are sharing your heart, the place where Jesus resides, and that is about the quickest and most intimate way for someone to know the real you. Being vulnerable with a friend gives you the ability to move right past the shallow end and straight up the ladder to the high dive.

Sure, vulnerability involves risk. Someone is going to see your flaws and fears when you decide to share the real stuff. But they will also see your dreams and hopes. Being honest about who you really are gives people a chance to see you, speak life over you when you need encouragement, and use words of warning when they see you heading in the wrong direction. These are the conversations that bring connection and trust that can withstand any life season . . . perhaps even bringing you closer through difficult ones.

THE GIFT OF GOING FIRST

Vulnerability takes a lot of confidence and self-assuredness. It can be scary to be vulnerable with someone because you are nervous they may not want to stay friends after hearing what you share. You may fear that you are too much of a burden for them if you ask them for help in a big way. Or, like me, you may be apprehensive to be seen as weak or imperfect.

It was the spring of my junior year of college. I had just left an on-campus dance party early (which is a warning sign that it was a bad time; I hear the phrase *dance party* and drop everything to show off my best moves). When I arrived at the party, I bopped around, literally, to different friend groups with acquaintances I had made from class or people I had studied abroad with the year before . . . but after about fifteen minutes of trying to fit in, I gave up. Feeling super defeated, I landed on my dorm's front lawn and just stared at the stars, wondering what was up with me. I even allowed some tears to trickle down my face. Everyone else was at the party. No one would see me.

To my surprise, a gal from the next dorm over was walking by and stopped when she saw me. I quickly sat up and plastered a smile on my face. She asked how I was doing and how my year was going thus far. "Fine," I told her. Then I asked her the same questions.

She paused for a moment.

"You know . . . things have been really hard this year," she said finally. "Homework feels really tough, and I am trying to balance that with sorority commitments. And I have really been struggling with loneliness."

Wait. Did she just say she was lonely?

I sat up a little straighter.

And with a little more confidence this time, I said, "You know, I've been feeling lonely this year too. It's weird, right?"

Her straightforwardness gave me the chance to express how I really felt. She gave me the gift of being honest first so I could have the room to be honest with her.

This newfound courage and mutual understanding led me to ask: "How about every time we feel lonely, we text each other, and we can go eat in the cafeteria together or study in the library side by side? And how about we go get milkshakes next weekend?"

She said yes. It was the start of a real friendship. One where I didn't have to pretend to be someone else because

I had already given my new friend a glimpse at my biggest weakness, and she still accepted me.

Vulnerability often normalizes the things we feel most ashamed about because we realize we are more alike than different.

EARNING VULNERABILITY

A lot of us put up caution tape around our hearts when we hear the word *vulnerability* because somewhere down the friendship road, someone abused our vulnerability. Maybe a tender truth we shared was used against us. Or perhaps someone shamed us when we told them about our struggle. Instead of receiving the love and forgiveness we hoped for, we were punished and manipulated. When vulnerability is used as a weapon, we often vow to never share our heart again.

Your vulnerability is precious and should never be used against you. But deep and meaningful relationships cannot be formed without it. Is there a way to determine how to offer vulnerability in ways that will lead to life and encouragement?

Yes. Vulnerability is a gift that should be freely given, but you get to choose when, how, and to whom you give it. First, to understand what kind of friend deserves this right, consider the list of friendship qualities you wrote back in chapter

2. What do you need to have in a friendship in order to break down your wall and show up fully?

Second, lean on the Holy Spirit, who provides us with discernment "to distinguish good from evil."[3] Yes, I am using the word *evil* here. Some women make mistakes in friendship but are still on your side; other women act in evil ways and are actively against you.

We must be prayerful about who we can trust to invite into the deep end of the friendship pool—because when you find yourself in seasons where you are drowning, some women will grab your hand to keep you from sinking, and others will enjoy watching you flail.

And third, ask yourself: Has this person earned the right to know? Does she mutually share real struggles? Is she "quick to hear, slow to speak, slow to anger"?[4] Is she attentive and compassionate when you confess sin, or is she withdrawn and harsh with her words? Proverbs 18:24 says, "A man of many companions may come to ruin, but there is a friend who sticks closer than a brother." This is who we are looking for—the person who is willing to stick around when things heat up and you can no longer hide your sweat stains.

Not everyone—not even wonderful, nice people—needs to know your sin and speak into it. That's not a right every person should have. Nor is it healthy. Inviting people to speak into your life is a privilege. Select wisely, pray for guidance, and take baby steps into vulnerability if you need to.

And as your friend shares her heart in return, know that you are responsible to protect what she shares. Nothing separates friends faster than gossip.[5] Guard your friend's words the way you want your words to be guarded.

TRANSFORMATION PARTNERS

The real goal of vulnerability is cultivating space for transformation. As followers of Jesus, we are called to spur one another on toward becoming more like Christ. God uses our friendships to help us see our faults, receive instruction, be strengthened by His Word, and find accountability.

Paul describes this relationship amid the community of Jesus in Ephesians 4. As he describes unity in the body of Christ, Paul says that gifts are given to each believer so we can all attain a oneness of faith and knowledge of Jesus, so that

> we may no longer be children, tossed to and fro
> by the waves and carried about by every wind of
> doctrine, by human cunning, by craftiness in deceitful
> schemes. Rather, speaking the truth in love, we are
> to grow up in every way into him who is the head,
> into Christ, from whom the whole body, joined

and held together by every joint with which it is
equipped, when each part is working properly, makes
the body grow so that it builds itself up in love.

EPHESIANS 4:14-16

Speaking the truth in love, we will all grow together—
and upward toward Jesus. Mutual maturation is good for
the whole body. Years ago our small group's mission state-
ment was, "You matter here." We wanted to remind people
that we can only go as far as every person is willing to go. If
we wanted to experience spiritual transformation, then each
person needed to commit to being vulnerable. Each person's
input mattered to the growth of the entire community. We
each have to show up in our friendships for vulnerability to
really work its magic.

If we do everything we can to conceal all the less-than-
shiny things about us, then no one can walk alongside us and
encourage us along the way.

But when we expose our weaknesses and allow our friends
to stand alongside us, then we no longer are tossed by the
winds of false truth and the schemes of people who will
prey on our vulnerabilities. We will be strong because our
friendships—which are guided by Jesus—will hold us up.

My church used to call friends like these "transformation

partners": two to three people whom you met with regularly to ask and answer the tough questions. Everyone agreed beforehand that this was not a casual get-together but a divine appointment where love *and* accountability was expected. It was a comfortable environment to confess sin and receive love and instruction.

As intimidating as accountability and confession may sound, these types of relationships are where I have seen some of the best growth in my life. Our meetings healed wounds, made me take responsibility for my sin, and gave me the extra nudge when I was too afraid to right wrongs otherwise.

We would also pray together, and I felt like I had two warriors beside me, fighting my battles with their words.

James 5:16 says, "Therefore, confess your sins to one another and pray for one another, that you may be healed. The prayer of a righteous person has great power as it is working."

A weekly habit of confession and prayer with these friends was powerful—but only because I was honest, only because I allowed these friends to *see* me.

You may or may not venture into a formal transformation-partner relationship, but every meaningful friendship should have the qualities of this intimate relationship. Vulnerability is key to caring for our friends in the most important areas of their lives—and key to allowing our friends to care for us in our most important areas.

We can't love our friends if we don't *know* them.

BE ALL THERE

Vulnerability means choosing to be *all there* with our friends. This means asking good questions and being intentional listeners. If you feel like you aren't good at either (and I often feel that way myself!), then take notes. Before I meet with a friend, sometimes I think about some questions I want to ask them. Often when I'm with a friend, we get into our groove of talking about the same things and rehashing the same stories that I completely blank or chicken out on asking the deep questions I really want to ask. To help yourself get to the important things, think of questions and write them down in your phone. You can casually glance at them as a reminder without making your conversation inauthentic.

Listening well also means following up on the things your friend has shared. Again, make notes of important work dates, anniversaries, doctor appointments, prayer requests—and follow up. This is a small but BIG step in making a friend feel like family.

And sometimes being "all there" in a friendship means being physically present. We put down our phones and sit with them as they share the hard things going on in their lives. In return, we need to be open when we need prayer or advice or together time. Friends don't see how much we need them if we don't communicate what we need. Friends are not mind readers. They won't show up on your doorstep with your favorite food because they magically intuited that you had a bad day. Sometimes, you just need to ask for a friend to listen and be there (and of course, bring ice cream).

Friendship Tip: If you are at a loss for great questions to go deep in a conversation, go to Google. Let someone else do the hard work for you. There are thousands of articles on "good questions to get to know people better," and one of them is bound to be a good fit for you. Another idea to connect more intentionally with a friend? Ask them to do a Bible study with you. There are many resources that build in questions and time for prayer. This is great for going deeper in your faith together without feeling like you need to force the conversation.

Celebrate Uniqueness

Friendship comes in all shapes and sizes . . .

and it never has to look the same way twice.

Your friendships don't have to be a carbon copy of the ones you see "over there" or the ones you've had in the past.

Each friendship holds its own unique personality—one that brings out a distinct side of you, a piece of you that shines when you are together.

As you craft each friendship, it would be almost impossible to get two that look exactly alike.

Let's celebrate the different ways each friend is the best at something instead of comparing one friendship to the next.

It is the different personalities and interests that make each friend special to another.

TOGETHER IS A BEAUTIFUL PLACE

I raise my glass for a toast, looking around the table at the new and old friends gathered. Faces stare back at me with smiles. I may have never chosen these women on my own, but God brought them into my life, into this family that He made.

And together is where I want to be on this special day. We've escaped our buzzing phones, our messy homes, and our long to-do lists. We have come to sit and savor the conversation.

It's my birthday, one of my favorite days of the year

because it gives me an excuse to gather my gals and thank them for making the previous year so meaningful.

In this moment, I feel joy, contentment, and sisterly love. But it is just a moment—a gift from God in the many moments that make up friendship. Because even with all our good intentions and godly love, at the end of the day, friendships still fall short.

I have spent countless hours living, breathing, and researching godly friendship. Little pink-Jelly-wearing Bailey has learned a lot in the last twenty-some years. But I still get it wrong. I still find myself in friendship conflict, afraid to confront something or feeling shame for the way I let a friendship go. There are plenty of moments I allow my task-oriented nature to overcome my love for people and steamroll a conversation just so we can move on to the next activity. I struggle with being a good friend every day.

And I understand that we'll still get stuck in unhealthy friendship patterns. We're going to walk through more rejection and uncomfortable social settings. We will struggle when friendships grow apart. Feelings will be hurt. And yet we will *still* be called to "lay down our lives" for imperfect people.

This is God's plan for my life, for your life, for every single one of us:

that they may all be one, just as you, Father, are in me, and I in you, that they also may be in us, so that the world may believe that you have sent me.

JOHN 17:21

After all the mistakes made, Jesus still prays for us to be His hands and feet—to pursue people with His intentional, transforming love. As we go out and make new friends, say hello to our neighbor for the first time, write a note to our cousin, bring cookies to the office, or join a Bible study, God will use our steps of obedience to create the intimate friendships we long for.

How do I know this?

Because every time I have trusted God and extended the olive branch of friendship, I have seen the lasting, life-giving fruit of being together.

So I'm asking you to be brave—to become a person who brings people together.

Be a friend who *invites* women into friendship and welcomes the risk.

Be a friend even when it's unpopular, time-consuming, or scary.

Be a friend even when your previous friendships didn't end so well.

Be a friend even when you feel like you're still figuring out what you want in a friend.

If each of us began to love just a few friends in our corner of the world, then a ripple effect of healthy, godly friendships would slowly transform our larger communities. God's love would stretch beyond our homes, beyond our Bible studies, and beyond our church buildings. It's the kind of belonging that draws people who are hungry and searching for true communion with God to the community of Jesus.

And when the ministry of friendship gets tough and you start to feel loneliness creep back in, come back to your first friendship, with the One who loves you most, for strength.

When you feel tired, come back to your first friendship for rest.

When you feel forgotten, judged, or hurt, come back to your first friendship for truth.

God has created a respite for you in Him.

So, for those of you who are closing this book, wondering when it will be your turn for a "perfect" friendship—remember that perfect is still to come:

[God said,] "Behold, the dwelling place of God is with man. He will dwell with them, and they will be his people, and God himself will be with them as their God. He will wipe away every tear form their eyes, and death shall be no more, neither shall there be mourning, nor crying, nor pain anymore, for the former things have passed away.

". . . Behold, I am making all things new."

REVELATION 21:3-5

John the disciple is describing above the scene of God's people dwelling in Zion, the new heaven and new earth. Zion was a physical place, King David's city,[1] but now it is a spiritual place where Christ will reign as King forever.[2] Zion is where God's people will live together in the presence of God: "the LORD has chosen Zion; he has desired it for his dwelling place."[3] This will be a place of "everlasting joy" and peace,[4] and all our relational insecurity will be met as we spend forever with God in Zion.

In this beautiful place, our friendship mistakes won't exist, and neither will the pain that we carry. God will make all things new, including our relationships.

We will all be **together** in perfect union and fellowship.

Our lasting friendship will become *everlasting* friendship.

So, as we wait for our future Zion, may we fight for togetherness instead of creating more room for division. May we use our gifts to pour into our people, helping one another grow closer to Jesus, instead of getting caught up in the pettiness of shallow connections.

And as you go through the inevitable ups and downs of your friendships, you can return to this book and remember the promises you made to yourself to be a Jesus-like friend. When you jump into a new season and need to create new friendship habits, come back to these ideas and gentle nudges to make time for finding and growing your friendships. I often have to give myself pep talks over and over to remind me of the importance of my ministry as a friend—to press on despite the enemy's attempts to stop me.

As I finish my toast and take a seat among my friends, I am reminded of all the simple, ordinary moments that led to these rich relationships.

What may have felt uncomfortable, awkward, or new at the time pales in comparison to the connections that we've built.

And that's just it. Right now, figuring out who your true friends are, navigating different seasons of life, and making time for each other feels challenging. But prioritizing your people is where true companionship is found. This is also where God can be found—in relationship. Each of you represent an aspect of His character. God's care, God's peace, God's love is what I see when I look out at my table of friends. Some I have known for five years; some for only five months. Some are married, some single; some have kids, and some hope to have kids. We are all so different. Yet each woman's story provides me with more reasons to thank God, to worship and praise Him.

Each of you brings something to the world that is meant to be shared. The body of Jesus works best when it is working together.

Your friendships matter.

You, as a friend, matter to your people.

In choosing to go through life together, you see that God's rich work and your worship grows in the gift of friendship.

I don't want this dinner party to end because I am so filled up in this moment.

But it will end.

And one day I will forget what we ate and the dress I chose for the occasion. Some of these friends will remain a memory (and some better be texting me inside jokes from their respective nursing homes).

I won't remember what was said or the stories we laughed about.

I'll only remember that we were together.

And together, with God, is a beautiful place to be.

ACKNOWLEDGMENTS

I was seventeen years old, sitting in my friend's basement, watching *America's Best Dance Crew*, when the conversation turned from wanting to quit school to become international pop-and-lock dancers to how special our friendships had become. How many friend groups gathered midweek to watch a hip-hop dance competition in costume? Right then and there, I vowed to one day write a book about how important and life-changing friendships centered on Jesus could be. Many of the *Friend-Date Ideas* in this book were created with this group of people. They changed me forever. I cannot give enough praise to God for ordaining such incredible friendships in such an influential time in my life. This book was originally inspired by this friend group. Wichita Cronies: I am forever indebted to your kindness, loyalty, and love.

Thank you, Jesus, for making a way for us to experience the best friendship on the planet. Through your sacrifice, we may all know the richness of intimate friendship with God.

Thank you, Tim, for cheering me on from the start as I pursued this dream. You have been my champion when I wanted to give up. Not only do you support my writing but you also support my ministry for friendship. You are my ultimate partner for loving people and inviting them in.

Thank you, Mom and Dad, for being an example of hospitality and kindness. You never met a stranger and always made room for someone at the table. You also have helped support me in this journey, and I can't thank you enough—I wouldn't be here without you.

Thank you, Lauren Kirk, for being a capital-*F* friend. Your friendship was more than sleepovers and funny videos. It brought me into the center of your love for Jesus, and it drew me into finding Jesus' love for myself. You are a true example of a godly friend who uses her friendship powers to bring others to Jesus.

Thank you, Denver community, for being a place for me to land as I figured out adult friendship. Thank you for doing life with me these last many years. You have made my life rich.

Thank you, Dan Balow, Bob Hostetler, and the Steve Laube Agency for believing in me and seeing something in me.

Thank you, Natalie Coulter, for being my first "freditor" (friend editor). I would not have made it this far without your insight and edits on this project and many others.

Thank you, Caitlyn Carlson, Don Pape, and the NavPress team, for being excited with me every step of the way and making this message for friendship tangible for readers.

Thank you, Robyn Field, Kelsey Chapman, Ann Swindell, Brooke Bohinc, and Noelle Rhodes, for being partners in the writing business. Your eyes on my writing, your business expertise, and your encouragement gave me the tools I needed to make it across the finish line.

Thank you to everyone who has supported me online—you know who you are. You walked with me from the very beginning: reading blogs, sharing posts, and initiating godly friendship right in your corner of the world. You are a true inspiration. This book is written with you in mind, and I hope you found the encouragement you needed to keep fighting for faithful friendship.